THE
TEEN SEX TRADE
MY STORY

THE TEEN SEX TRADE

MY STORY

Jade H. Brooks

Formac Publishing Company Limited
Halifax

Formac Publishing Company Limited recognizes the support of the Province of Nova Scotia through the Department of Communities, Culture and Heritage. We are pleased to work in partnership with the Province of Nova Scotia to develop and promote our cultural resources for all Nova Scotians. We acknowledge the support of the Canada Council for the Arts, which last year invested $153 million to bring the arts to Canadians throughout the country. This project has been made possible in part by the Government of Canada.

Cover design: Tyler Cleroux
Cover image: iStock

Library and Archives Canada Cataloguing in Publication

Brooks, Jade H., author
      The teen sex trade : my story / Jade H. Brooks.

Issued in print and electronic formats.
ISBN 978-1-4595-0499-8 (softcover).--ISBN 978-1-4595-0500-1 (EPUB)

      1. Brooks, Jade. 2. Child trafficking victims--Canada--Biography.
3. Human trafficking victims--Canada--Biography. 4. Child prostitutes--
Canada--Biography. 5. Child trafficking--Canada. 6. Human
trafficking--Canada. 7. Teenage prostitution--Canada. 8. Prostitution--
Canada. I. Title.

HQ281.B766 2017   364.15'34092   C2017-903290-9
                                                       C2017-903291-7

Formac Publishing Company Limited
5502 Atlantic Street
Halifax, Nova Scotia, Canada
B3H 1G4
www.formac.ca

Printed and bound in Canada.

For my children —
Understand that it took all of this for me to be all
that I am now. I have no regrets. I hold no grudges.
My hope is that you love and honor yourselves and
each other, as well as your father and me — so much
so that to break someone's spirit is incomprehensible.

PREFACE

When I started writing this book in April 2015, it wasn't with a particular goal in mind. A suggestion from a friend was what led me to begin writing. I'd shared my story with him, in a nutshell. I'd told him I was your typical girl who had had it rough as a child, met the wrong guy, fell in what I thought was love, had it go badly and now I was trying to put my life back together.

As we stood looking at each other through a video chat app, I shrugged off my experiences. I didn't think it was a big deal. But he did. He asked for more details and when I gave them to him, he was visibly angry. As a father of five boys, he couldn't fathom any of his sons treating a female in the way that I'd described. I didn't understand why he cared enough to be so upset. What happened to me happened all the time where I'm from. I hadn't known this man very long. He had a million questions and I did my best to answer them. Recalling certain memories still made my skin crawl.

When I finished telling him more of my story, he hit me with more compliments than I could handle. I stood there blushing. "You should write a book," he said. "I don't know about that," I replied. He went on to tell me how I'm a survivor and that people need to hear my story. "You could save someone's life," he told me. I'd never thought about it in that way. I just wanted to put the memories behind me — erase them. I didn't feel like a survivor. I told him I'd think about it and he promised to keep reminding me until I started writing (which he did).

Eventually, I grew tired of hearing him talk about it, but I didn't know where to begin. I sat there with a pen in my hand and a new notebook that I'd gotten for my birthday that year. *What's your first memory?* I asked myself.

From there, I wrote as much as I could until my hand stiffened. I knew I'd have to pace myself if I was going to see this through until the end, though I didn't see an end in sight at that time. On top of writing, I was in college full time and exams were quickly approaching. About a month after I started writing this, I got into a huge argument with the family friend I was staying with. The argument was nothing but a difference in opinion, but judging by its magnitude and how emotionally charged it led me to be, I knew that it was time for me to leave after living with them for two years.

I had nowhere to go, so I packed some clothes in a duffel bag and made a few calls to find a homeless shelter. The closest one that had a bed available was more than an hour away. I was exhausted just thinking about what I had to do. I'd never been to a shelter before. I didn't know what I was walking into. Images of dozens of people in one room, lying on blankets on the floor, flooded my mind. *Would it be like how it is on TV?* I wondered. I grabbed my notebook, more out of fear of someone reading it than intending to continue writing. From the moment I entered the shelter, I pretty much decided to forget about everyone and everything and just disappear for a while to get my head together. Aside from assuring a few of my family members and friends that I was alive, I didn't think I deserved anyone's time or conversation. I was homeless. I had nothing to offer. I managed to finish my last few weeks of college. I was only working a couple of times a week and then my work slowed to a halt. I had no money and nothing to do. With so much time on my hands and boredom consuming me, I figured I might as well write.

There are many words to describe what writing that summer was like — challenging, exhausting, re-traumatizing, maddening, confusing . . . I purged all of the memories from that time in my life when I was with my first serious boyfriend, and from all of the years that had led up to that time. Some days I could write ten pages with little regard to what they meant. Other days, I would have to stop because I'd become so angry. I was angry at him for putting me through so much and angry at myself for being stupid enough to allow him to. Occasionally, I'd get a couple of pages written and have to stop because I found myself missing him and I couldn't understand why. I'd think about the men I'd seen after him and how I'd convinced myself that those relationships had failed because it was him who I was meant to be with, despite everything that had happened. I hated myself for thinking like that. *How could I be so foolish?* I asked myself. It didn't help that alongside my most violent memories of him were fond memories of us laughing, going on dates and making love. It was a tiring and confusing phenomenon, but I continued writing.

His name alone made me cringe. Seeing it written over and over was too much for me to bear sometimes. At one point, I kept a tally of how many times I wrote his name until I forced myself to stop. I thought it would serve as a basis for a good poem later on, but it became daunting. I decided to give him a pseudonym that seemed more fitting than the name I'd used for so many years. Not only did I believe karma would come back around for him but it coincided with a phrase he'd embedded into my brain from the time we entered *the Game*. "You get out what you put in," he told me when I asked him how long we would have to do it for. And so he became *Carma*.

Long after I started documenting these experiences, which was very much like an extended diary of past times, I debated with myself whether or not I would use people's real names in the event that my book got published. There were a few questions that I had to ask myself in order to come to a final decision. *What would be my purpose in sharing this book publicly? Who does it serve to use people's real names?* The most important question was, *am I prepared for the consequences of this book going public whether I use real names or not?* I kept my real name because, well, I'm me.

My purpose in sharing this book publicly is to educate people, particularly young women. The communities I was raised in have a long, long history of engaging in this lifestyle. For generations, women have been targeted, manipulated, abused and sold for the profit of another; many of them didn't know what they were signing up for, if they had signed up at all. Women have been and still are being physically kidnapped and confined into this industry. Young women in my community, including myself, have seen this lifestyle glamourized for so long that it's become engrained in us as normal. All of the stories I'd heard as a teenager and beyond about stripping and pimping had desensitized me so much that I didn't realize there could be more to the story. I didn't have anyone around to tell me that it *wasn't* normal for a man to convince his girlfriend that she needed to sell her body in order to prove her love or have a life worth living. So I share this book publicly for the women who didn't get to choose and for those who may get to a point where they have to choose. I want them to know that they do have a choice, even when they don't feel like they do. If they find themselves attempting to pick up the pieces of their life as I had to do, I want them to know there is life beyond it.

While using real names would have saved me a lot of time and frustration during the writing of this and in working with my editor, I decided against it. It didn't serve my wellbeing to use real names. I figured that either way, the story would get out there and those who knew would know. If there is any soul or conscience in the men who have harmed me or the women who stood by and witnessed this harm (knowingly and unknowingly), then they would have to deal with those feelings accordingly. I have already forgiven those people from that time in my life.

My purpose is not to expose individuals. These young men and women could have been anyone. In my mind, it doesn't serve these people to have their involvement in my pain stamped with their real names. The affected communities deserve to decide for and amongst themselves how they will hold each other accountable. Me ostracizing individuals by naming their names to the worlds they've come to know and the one beyond does not serve their wellbeing or their community's ability to heal from generations of this cycle of abuse. It certainly doesn't allow us to go back in time and undo the harm that was done. Instead, I intend for this book to serve as a catalyst for community discussion on how we can come together and combat the root of this crime. Prevention is the best measure. Intervention is much more complex. With tools like awareness, accountability and willingness to be vulnerable, we can heal our young women *and men*. But nothing will change if we don't even acknowledge that something needs to change.

Now, am I prepared for the consequences of this book being published? Honestly, I don't know. A few women have expressed their concern for my safety upon releasing this book. I empathize with them. I've already received threats from men connected to the Game in various capacities through the grapevine. The possibilities of what could happen are endless. I cannot prepare for what I don't know, I can only be cautious. At the same time, I must walk in my truth and I'm prepared to risk whatever the consequences may be in order to honour that walk. Maybe I've underestimated or romanticized the seriousness of what it means to publish this book. As a poet, I tend to view the world around me through a lens that is very different than that of someone more logical; nonetheless, the process has been well worth it.

* * *

It's hard to explain how I was able to recall all of the experiences described in these pages solely from memory. Even I was surprised by my ability to remember. I thought I'd forgotten a lot of it because I'd forced myself to repress the memories for so long. My early childhood was one of the hardest things to remember. For some of the details, I had to double check with my sisters. The years following my time with Carma, I achieved this repression by distracting myself with men, partying and throwing my all into an education I wasn't even sure I wanted. To some extent, it was even achieved by convincing myself that one day when Carma was tired of the fast life and ready to love me, he would come back to me. I fantasized about that for quite some time. The more I remembered and penned in my notebooks, the more I realized I needed to write this — for others and for myself. Little by little, the memories unlocked themselves from the places in my brain where they were stored and I could play out entire scenes in my head where I was being yelled at, lectured or reassured. Most memories appeared as clearly as if I was watching an HD movie in my mind. Others were blurry and I made it a point to name those instances as well. I also created a timeline of events as I went along so that I made sure not to forget any of the things I wanted to include.

It's important to say here that this isn't an account of my *entire* life. I mean, I couldn't remember every single detail from childhood to present and some of it wasn't relevant to my truth of what led me to Carma (and to stay with him). But I have given you, the reader, all that I could to paint a picture of how a girl like me could get pulled into this world of abuse and sex despite having always been "so smart" as so many often point out — and often not in an admiring way.

CHAPTER 1

CHILDHOOD

I come from a two-parent household, where I grew up alongside four of my eight siblings: Riley, my older brother, my older sisters Meghan and Quin and my younger brother Aaron. My other siblings are three older brothers and another older sister — my dad's children from other relationships. My dad tried to help us develop a relationship with our half-siblings, despite having different moms, but I mostly spent my time around the siblings I shared a house with.

We had chores that followed traditional gender roles — girls had to do the dishes and boys had to take out the garbage. Meghan, Quin and I rotated other household duties like switching the loads of laundry from washer to dryer then putting it away after my mom folded it. For the most part, I didn't think much of our chores except when I didn't want to do *any* chores. "Why can't Riley do the dishes?" I'd moan to my mom. "He just took out the garbage. Now go do the dishes!" she would yell.

We went to school every day. My mom wasn't fond of us missing any classes. I thought it was because she didn't want to hang out with us all day. My dad walked us to school and back for the majority of our elementary years. I loved school in those years, especially English. Writing came so naturally to me. I worked hard to perfect my penmanship and stay organized. We participated in after-school programs, March break activities and summer camps. My favourite programs were learning how to swim and skate. Mom went through great lengths to ensure we didn't mess up our newly straightened or braided hair, which she took the liberty of doing every week or so. Quin and I would often have to wear swim caps, but somehow my hair still managed to get wet. In addition to Mom styling our hair, she would perm it. I hated the process but loved my thin and silky hair once the perm was rinsed out. Still, I shrieked in terror every time it was time to get my hair done. "Your scalp ain't that sensitive!" Mom said as I'd pull my head away from the wooden popsicle stick she was using to apply the perm with. One afternoon, I screamed so hard that our upstairs neighbour came knocking on our door. "What are you doing to that child?" she demanded to know. "You better get off my doorstep! She is getting her hair braided, ain't nobody hurting that child!" Mom replied, with her eyes bulging. I was scolded for causing such a scene.

We went to the tutoring program on Tuesdays and Thursdays, even though I didn't really need a tutor. On Sundays, we attended Sunday school. I assume it was a Christian church, though I can't be positive. We sang songs

like "Jesus Loves the Little Children," but I never learned
to recite the Psalm 23. I wasn't particularly into the whole
church thing but I wasn't against it either. I got to see my
friends so it worked for me. I was very much an introvert.
I tried hard to fit in with my friends, and with Quin and
Aaron. If I had it my way, I would stay inside, lie down and
read all day but some days I wanted to be around my friends
or my mom would force me to go outside.

My neighbourhood was extremely small. Everyone knew
each other. And *everyone* knew my mom. She'd grown up in
Halifax and she had an infamous reputation for being a party
girl. Whenever she went to visit her friends or attend a party,
you heard her coming before you saw her. Her loud voice and
booming laugh was unlike any other. You either knew her for
her sometimes embarrassing party antics or her cooking. She
could create literally anything in the kitchen.

Within my hood, there were two small convenience
stores that all of the kids went to. One always had stale candy
but we went there anyway. The other had penny candy, cup
freezies and had a raspberry patch behind it. We weren't
allowed back there but we'd sneak behind the fence anyway
and collect raspberries.

The day we moved to our first townhome in Mulgrave
Park, my dad was so excited. I was five years old and we had
just moved to Nova Scotia from Toronto. Just to be funny,
he picked my mom up like a baby so that he could walk
her over the threshold to our new life. As my siblings and I
squealed beneath them, my dad pretended that my mom was
too heavy and she scoffed him off.

We all made a dash to pick a bedroom. Of course, there
weren't many options for us. It was a four-bedroom townhouse,
which meant my parents had their room, Quin and I shared

a room, my two brothers shared a room and my eldest sister, Meghan, had her own room.

Our first night there was cold. We didn't have anything except for a mattress on the floor and some blankets. My mom told everyone to sleep with socks on because there was a draft, though I wasn't too sure what a draft was. The mattress Quin and I shared was eventually upgraded to bunk beds and we fought over who would sleep on the top bunk. After a while, my dad came in with the good old "flip a coin" solution. Whoever won the coin toss claimed the top bunk and the loser got pink gum from the store that always sold stale products. Quin lost the coin toss and had to sleep on the bottom bunk where she was always kicking my mattress or lifting it up with her feet to be mean. When I got tired of that, I agreed to switch and let her have the top bunk, even though she'd already vandalized the underside of my bunk with pen and markers.

It was always like that between us. Although Quin and I were nearly the same height, she was much stronger than I was, and she still is. My mom would say, "Quin, stop manhandling your sister!" Quin's favourite name to insult me with was "beaver." She and Aaron were the main reason why I had insecurities about my small, spaced out teeth that I'd inherited from my father.

That was the reality of my childhood — sibling rivalry, going to school and attending after-school programs to stay out of my mom's hair.

The other reality was that my parents were very abusive toward each other. Some nights, my dad would stand on our front step, drunk and yelling at my mom to let him in. On those same nights, he'd see one of us in the window, crying because we wanted to let him into the house but we'd been instructed by our mother not to touch the lock or else we'd be in trouble. One night, I stood in the window of Meghan's bedroom, terrified, as I watched my mom and dad beat the shit out of each other for what seemed like the millionth time.

This night was particularly bad. It was well after sunset, but the parking lot lampposts lit our front steps where my parents were fighting. My dad was trying to put my mom out of the house while she was sloppy drunk, again. Each time he managed to get her to the bottom of the steps, she would crawl her way back up, cursing and screaming at my dad the entire time.

Her next effort would be her last; as she reached the top of the stairs, my dad pushed her and she went tumbling backward down the concrete steps. She tried to grab the railing but she couldn't. Her head hit the steps before her chin tucked into her chest. It was like a backward somersault.

"Mooom!" I screamed as she tumbled down the stairs.

As she fell, my dad's name rang through the air. "Leviiiii!" she screeched.

Her body lay at the bottom of the stairs, limp. *She's dead*, I remember thinking.

The rest of that night is a blur to me. I don't remember her getting up or if there was any blood. I vaguely remember the ambulance lights flashing in my sister's bedroom window, the room where I usually slept to feel at peace.

Although there are many, many things that I cannot (or will not) remember about my childhood, I remember the days when my parents didn't fight.

There were times when they loved and were playful — it was almost annoying. My mom's favourite war tactic was throwing cold water on my dad. Some days it was out of anger and some days they were like two teenagers in love, chasing each other through our one-level townhouse, having a water fight. Us kids would be jumping on the couch yelling and laughing, cheering them on. Eventually, my dad would give up and say, "Okay, Mugs!" That was his nickname for her. "I'm done! I'm not playing anymore!"

My mom was fierce but she would let him surrender. In those moments, I felt that my parents really did love each other somewhere beneath the fighting.

Still, I wondered why they put up with each other. Why did they beat the shit out of each other one day and sit down and watch a movie together the next? I figured that was just the way love was. It was confusing. I didn't understand why things got so bad. This wasn't some new relationship between two strangers. My parents had been together since they were young. They'd met when my mom was fifteen and my dad was twenty. They were together before she gave birth to Riley. When I was six months old, they got married. I'd seen the pictures; I was in them! They looked happy.

My mom and I weren't close at all, although from what I could see, she wasn't particularly close with any of us. At least, not in an affectionate way. I don't remember her hugging me or telling me that she loved me. Aaron received the most attention from her, as he was the youngest. He often got away with things like being allowed to leave the dinner table without finishing his food. "Leave the drumsticks for Aaron. You know he only likes the drumsticks," Mom would say whenever she cooked chicken. We'd all huff and puff that he got to choose what he wanted to eat. "It all tastes the same!" I'd exclaim. My mom usually stayed home while my dad went to work. She did her wifely duties by doing the majority of the cooking and cleaning. She took care *of* us but didn't take care *with* us. She yelled at us a lot, especially if we brought our mess from outdoors onto the kitchen floor that she always seemed to have just waxed. I think my mom was annoyed with us a lot. I rarely got in trouble, so it wasn't often that I was singled out with attention from her. Whenever I did get in trouble it was usually more along the lines of all of us taking the blame for what one of my siblings did.

One time I do remember getting in trouble.

The elementary school that my siblings and I attended was across the street from a huge church. The church had a small grassy hill that led to a metal fence on one side and a long set of stairs on the other. Instead of walking up the steps, my siblings' friends broke a hole in the fence and pulled it back so that the rest of us could walk through and take a shortcut.

Of course, our group was damaging property, but it didn't seem like a big deal. The group convinced each other that we could get away with it.

I was terrified but I did it anyway, because I didn't want my siblings and their friends to single me out for being the only one who was scared.

But then, as if on cue, we heard a teacher yell at us from across the street. Everyone ran!

Down the street, we laughed, trying to catch our breath. We thought we got away with it until we arrived at school the next day. The teacher had seen everything. She had a fresh detention form for each person who had gone through the fence — everyone except for me.

I didn't get detention but I did get a "yellow form," which was equivalent to a written warning before disciplinary action had to be taken. The reason I didn't immediately get detention was because the teacher knew I was a good student. It may have seemed like I got off the hook, but I think I was more afraid to tell my mom about the incident than I was when I got in trouble. I didn't want to get a beating or receive two weeks of grounding, but mostly I didn't want my mom to be mad at me, or worse, disappointed.

The teacher knew I had an above average reading record. My favourite books to read were the Nancy Drew series. She knew I was quiet. She also knew who my siblings were, and that they weren't bad kids but they were mischievous. They were adventurous. They were risk takers.

Once I got home from school that day, I decided to tell the truth about what happened. My mom had to tell me to stop and say my words properly because I was speaking so quickly. I showed her the form that she had to sign and told her that it wasn't my fault.

To my surprise, she responded very calmly.

She said, "Since you told the truth, you're not in trouble but don't let me see this happen again." I told her it wouldn't happen anymore and then I was free to go. With my "yellow form" signed, I went about the rest of my day with a huge grin on my face.

In many ways my childhood was like that of other kids: I got in trouble. I laughed. I read. I enjoyed myself.

There are even times I recall playing my parents against each other.

My dad would tell us that we weren't allowed outside directly after we finished eating our dinner. He claimed that we had to let our food settle first. Some nights, we would beg him to let us go outside. Our favourite line was, "Pretty, pretty please, Dad? With a cherry on top! We'll love you forever and ever!" Some nights he would cave and let us go and other nights he stood his ground. When the timing was right, on nights that he'd refuse to let us go, we would find my mom and ask her if we could go out, without telling her that Dad had already said no.

We probably got caught more often than not and were made to stay indoors, but some days my dad would pretend to be mad and chase us outside, saying, "Get outta here!" in a deep, grumbling voice.

We'd squeal and laugh, running in full sprint until we were a safe distance away. My dad was very playful at times, which makes me wonder now if there was any truth to the insult that my mom would spew at my dad when she was angry. "You and your bipolar ass!" she'd say.

"What does bipolar mean?" I asked once. "Ask your father!" Mom replied. "It means crazy! One minute he wants to carry on and the next minute he's trying to fight with somebody!"

My dad was a great dad. He would take us fishing on the Halifax Harbour. I was terrified to take the fish off the hook whenever I caught one. I also hated getting the fish scales on my hands and I hated the way the fish flopped around while out of the water.

A lot of people said we weren't supposed to eat the fish from the harbour because the water was so dirty but my mom was the ultimate chef. She knew how to clean fish, and we never got sick from it. A lot of our neighbours sent their food over for mom to cook and send back to them. By the time I was old enough to realize we were poor, I was amazed at how well we ate.

We didn't have Kraft Dinner and wieners for supper every night like some families. We ate chicken, fish, steak, pork chops, chili, spaghetti, vegetables, pasta, rice, you name it! I mean, sometimes if my mom was being lazy she would make us Kraft Dinner or soup, but mostly we ate home-cooked meals. We never missed a meal.

The best thing about having a functioning who also smoked weed alcoholic as a mother was that she was always *feeling* for something good to eat — but her munchies rarely consisted of chips and chocolate, it was more like steak and baked potatoes. She would make huge breakfasts on Saturdays or Sundays and whichever day she didn't cook, she would tell us that we better open up the cupboards and find ourselves something to eat.

In those instances, Meghan usually took over and cooked for us. Meghan was a pro at making pancakes, French toast and tuna melts. I was content with eating a can of cream-style corn for lunch but my mom would tell me that I wasn't allowed to only eat that.

Out of all of my siblings, Meghan was my favourite. Although she was a few years older than me, we could've easily passed as twins. Everyone knew she favoured me. I'd awaken from these terrible, recurring nightmares and walk to her room, peeking my head in the door. "Meghan, can I sleep in your room?" I'd ask. Usually she didn't question me. She'd just peel back her blanket and scoot over to make room for me. "Why can't you sleep in your own room?" she asked more than once. I guess sometimes she wanted to sleep alone. "I had a bad dream," I said. "What kind of dream?" she asked. I recounted the nightmare to her. It always started with a fight between my parents. I'd either be watching from a bird's eye view or standing near them on the stairs, helpless. I couldn't remember what the arguments were about. I only know that the two of them were raging, their veins popping out of their necks, eyes wide. It was as if they didn't see me standing there. All of a sudden, there was a knife in my dad's hand. He started stabbing my mom while I screamed at him to stop. Blood splattered everywhere.

He stabbed her repeatedly until she fell down the stairs and laid on the floor, bleeding out. I probably had these dreams a couple times per week. Every so often, I would get in between my parents and my dad would stab me by mistake in attempts to get to my mom. Then, I'd wake up in terror. It didn't take long for me to find my way into Meghan's room. Meghan didn't say much when I told her aside from reassuring me that it wasn't real. We always laid in the same position. She would be lying in a running position and the nook of her arm would be my pillow. It was with her that I found my comfort.

One thing Meghan hated about me was when I would wear her clothes without asking. "Mom, tell Jade to stay out of my room!" she would yell. Laughing to myself, I would sneak her shirt back into her room when she wasn't looking or while she was gone out. It wasn't my fault she had nice clothes and we were the same size. As Meghan got older, her free time went from being spent with me to being spent with her friends. It was a privilege to be invited to tag along and I loved it because her girl friends adored me. "Look at her, she's right cute!" Meghan's friends would say. I ate up the attention they gave me as they pulled me into tight hugs and touched the bobbles on my ponytails.

"You can go to the Square if you want," I said to Meghan one night while we were outside. I didn't want her to think I was holding her back from having fun, even though she wasn't supposed to go to the Square, a rule given by our parents. She and her friends gasped, while the guys all got loud at the same time. "I told you that's where you were going!" one boy yelled, still laughing. I didn't understand what the joke was. "Oh my god, Jade! I can't take you nowhere!" Meghan hollered. I still didn't get it. "The boys weren't supposed to know where we were going," she said. My cheeks burned with embarrassment. Meghan sent me home. I didn't get to hang out with them much after that, but I still viewed her as my best friend.

*   *   *

It was around the fourth grade or so when I started noticing boys. My first crush was named Raury. He was light-skinned with a curly brown afro and a big smile. He was bigger than me. He towered over me, actually. And he spit when he talked. I don't know what it was exactly that I liked about Raury, I just did. One day, we were leaving the after-school program that all of the hood kids attended. When it came time to part ways to go to our respective 'blocks,' he kissed me on the lips. All of our friends went crazy, laughing and teasing us. Quin and Aaron ran home and told on me but I denied it. "You wouldn't do that would ya, Jadey? You don't kiss boys, do ya?" Dad asked. "I would never," I replied sweetly. Aaron swore up and down that I was lying but my dad believed me.

When Raury first showed a jealous streak, I was more flattered than anything. One night, Quin came home from playing basketball at the community centre, all excited about something. "Jade, guess what! Raury and Tray were fighting over you!" Quin said. I felt a weird sense of happiness. They both had a crush on me! I wished I had seen the fight. I felt like a big deal in that moment.

Pretty soon, Raury's violence was turned toward me, even though we were so young. We had gotten into an argument on the school playground and I threatened to rip up his class photo that he'd signed and given to me as a gift. Over and over, he warned me not to do it. I looked at him with defiance and did it anyway. He watched as I shredded the picture to pieces and they fell all over the rocky platform beneath the jungle gym.

As fast as I could blink, he slapped me across the face. His hands were huge, so you know it was a hefty smack. I have no recollection of what happened to him after he hit me. I assume there were no consequences. I don't know if I told on him or how I felt afterward.

That same year, I started crushing on another guy in my class. His name was Amir. Every girl had a crush on this guy and he didn't like any of us back. The one girl who didn't like him was the one he wanted, of course. Her name was Breanne. Unlike us, with our kinky braids and brown skin, Breanne was light-skinned with freckles and hair that was long, brown, straight and silky. We considered that to be "good" hair. Her hair was nothing like ours with all of its knots and tendencies to get fuzzy with the least bit of moisture.

All of us girls crowded around the basketball court at recess to watch Amir play. Our fourth grade class would have gym outside and he was our first target in games like dodgeball and red rover. Our team of girls would be chanting, "Red rover, red rover, we call AMIR over!"

He wasn't crushing on me by any means, but there were instances when I found myself alone with him. The whole gang of us hung out — Quin, Aaron, Amir, his brother and I — and sometimes it was just the two of us after everyone else had gone in the house for the night. We'd sit on this wooden box near his place or toss the basketball around in his backyard, where his brother had installed a basketball net. I don't remember talking about anything in particular but I was happy just to be with him. Once, a girl from our school walked past and saw us sitting together. "Aww, look at you two!" she teased. Amir quickly brushed it off, saying we were just friends. I stayed quiet but smiled to myself. Even though he had dismissed the idea, I was surprised and pleased that anyone would think I had a chance with him.

His mom was always calm and collected when we'd knock on their door and ask if Amir was allowed outside. But, like all other moms in the hood, she didn't take any shit. When Amir was grounded, she made sure to let us know. There wasn't anything shy about her! On those days, when Amir wasn't allowed outside, he would peek his head out of his bedroom window and talk to us until his mom would holler at him to stop.

I think the reason why almost all of the girls liked Amir was because he was *that* guy. He was light-skinned with brown eyes, just the right height and he had that "good" hair, much like Breanne had. Things like that were admired amongst us.

For me, it was because of the way he made me laugh. He was funny. I mean, *really* funny — like a young Chris Rock.

To make him even more perfect, he did a great impression of Chris Tucker in the movie *Rush Hour*. I often daydreamed that he liked me back. He was easily the best looking and most popular guy in our class, probably even in our whole grade.

I found myself wondering why he liked Breanne when she didn't like him back and he could, essentially, have any girl he wanted. I don't like to admit it but the other girls and I naturally disliked Breanne. Here she was getting all of Amir's attention when she didn't even like him. On top of that, another (light-skinned) guy (with pretty green eyes) was giving her *more* attention that she didn't want. How dare she?

Throughout our elementary years, we were already conscious and jealous of skin colour. It got worse around ages eight and nine when we started to be attracted to each other, competing to be noticed. I would walk around and try to avoid swinging my arms in my eye's path so that I wouldn't have to think about how dark I was. I was teased a lot about my complexion, teeth and hair. I was teased for being dark-skinned and I teased people who were darker than me, especially Aaron. My siblings and I called him names like blacky, darky sparky and underdog.

I was almost ten years old when my parents' marriage had reached its breaking point. My mom moved out and got her own townhouse on Creighton Street, near Uniacke Square. For whatever reason, Aaron, Quin, Meghan and I had to leave our dad's house and go live with our mom. We didn't get to make this decision for ourselves. Or at least, I didn't. Life changed when we moved. We'd attended the same school forever. Even Meghan and Riley went to St. Joseph's A. McKay. Suddenly, we were forced into Joseph Howe Elementary, which was in my mom's new neighbourhood. It was an upgrade from our single storey townhome. This townhouse was big and freshly painted. I still shared a room with Quin but we had huge ceiling-length windows and two bathrooms. My mom wasn't nearly as enthusiastic a parent as my dad. She was often out with her girl friends, drinking or doing her own thing at home. My mom and I still weren't close at all so I was thankful for Quin and especially for Aaron's ability to make friends quickly at this time. Being in a new neighbourhood, I just hung out with them and whoever. It didn't take long for us to begin hanging out with a group of kids that lived on our block. I was really into basketball. The girl friends that I made played alongside me at the community YMCA. Our team was called the Panthers. We were a pretty solid team, holding more wins than losses. I was a shooting guard. I was pretty good but definitely not WNBA material. It was fun and gave me time to be around my best girls, but eventually I tired of the game and preferred to hang outside with my new friends, one of whom was Nikko.

I met Nikko the summer before he was to enter grade six and I was to enter grade five. Nikko was light-skinned with long, dark brown hair and brown eyes, like Amir. Almost instantly, I took a liking to him. Nikko and I became sweethearts. We were always together.

He was very close to his family and lived with his mom, his two aunts and three cousins. They spent a lot of time together and so I began to spend time with them too. Nikko was a true artist if I ever knew one. He had a talent for drawing and would make me these complex, graffiti-type pictures that bore my name in the middle.

Sometimes, they said "sweetheart" or his nickname, which was "Neeks." There were times when we spent entire days drawing together on his living room floor.

I thought I was a pretty decent artist, nothing like him, but I could recreate characters pretty well, and so I began trying to imitate his work. I would try to do graffiti but it always came out looking like a maze.

Naturally, we were teased all the time about being "love birds" and we were exactly that. If I happened to be around at supper time and there wasn't enough food to go around, he would share his with me. He was nice like that. Although he and his mom had a close relationship, sometimes he would speak disrespectfully toward her when he didn't get his way. There were a few times when his disrespect came because she wouldn't let me come over for whatever reason.

I remember the feeling I had the day Nikko came over to my house for lunch. I was so worried that my mom would do or say something embarrassing, whether she was drunk or sober. Thankfully, she didn't. I was very relieved.

The chill-out spot at those times was in the basement of a girl named Kya, who had house parties every weekend. Everyone would be in there bumpin' and grindin', except for me. While the girls had their hands on their waists and knees with their butts pressed against the guys, I was standing against the wall either by myself or with Nikko.

I was painfully shy, a wallflower. As far as labels go, I was one of the "green" girls. This basically translated to being "afraid" to do sexual stuff with guys. It wasn't that I was afraid to — I wanted to, especially with Nikko, but my shyness held me back.

This shyness was tested one evening in the basement of Nikko's best friend, Angel. Angel brought ice cream downstairs for the three of us as we sat squeezed together on a big, comfy chair. "As a joke," they both pounced on me. One of them was holding my arms while the other grabbed my boobs. I was very uncomfortable but they were laughing, so I tried to laugh too. All the while, I was squirming and holding my chest, trying to get out from under their grip. It was an isolated incident. They were pretty respectful after that and Nikko and I were still inseparable.

That summer went pretty smoothly. The two of us, along with Quin, Aaron, Angel and whoever else tagged along often went to the Commons, a community swimming pool, park and skateboarding area. We ran around the neighbourhood as children our age would do.

We spent weekends with my dad, back in Mulgrave Park. I had a friend there named Laila. Laila's mom spent most of her time lying on her living room couch in the dark, so sometimes on the weekends Laila would be shipped off to visit with her cousins, near my dad's house. I was at a sleepover with her and her cousins when I noticed a bump near my bikini line. I pushed on it and it hurt really badly. I had no idea that this bump was only the first sign of a more serious skin condition that would cause me bigger problems later. I began to cry and everyone kept on asking me what was wrong, but I didn't want to tell them. All I said was that I wanted to go home. They tried to calm me down and convince me to stay until Laila's aunt finally came into the room. She asked me what was wrong and I was hesitant to show her, especially in front of my friends. We went into the bathroom and I showed her the lump. She tried to soothe me as she called my mom. I went home teary eyed, not wanting to go to sleepovers ever again.

Often I didn't want to go anyway, because it meant being away from Nikko.

My mom would scorn me for not wanting to spend time with my dad. It wasn't like I could call Nikko under my dad's watchful eye, and I definitely couldn't text him because I didn't have a cellphone back then.

Having Laila there made it not so boring, but I would miss Nikko each weekend and spring back to him the first chance I got on Sunday evening or Monday morning. At least that's how it went until the day I found a crack pipe in my mom's kitchen drawer.

CHAPTER 2

IN THE SYSTEM

By this time, summer had ended and school had started up again. I was in grade five at Joseph Howe Elementary. I was there with Aaron who was in grade four and Quin who was in grade six.

At first, I had no idea that what I'd found in the kitchen drawer was a crack pipe. It was a clear, glass contraption with a little bowl at the top and a hole in one end. The little bowl was blackened from something. I asked Meghan what it was for. She said, "Don't be surprised if Children's Aid comes and takes you guys." Then, as if it was something to be taken lightly, she scoffed and walked away coldly, leaving me standing in the kitchen alone. I couldn't tell if she was angry or annoyed with me, so I just put the pipe back into the drawer.

A couple of weeks later, Quin, Aaron and I went to school like any other regular day. Then, just before the end of the day, we were called to the office. When we got there, my dad was waiting for us. We ran to greet him. He was with a plump lady about our mom's age. She was very pretty with green eyes, freckles and a businesslike demeanor. I noticed that she dressed very well. She matched all over in a skirt and blouse, and her toes were perfectly painted. My dad was very somber. We all piled into the lady's car as my dad explained that we were going to my cousin Whitney's house. Whitney lived by my dad in Mulgrave Park.

Once we got there, my dad sat us all down together in one of the bedrooms and his next words were choppy as he cleared his throat too many times. Tears streamed down his face as he tried not to stutter — something he does whenever he is mad. This time, he wasn't speaking out of anger. I don't think I'd ever seen my dad cry before that. "You guys are gonna stay with Cousin Whitney for a while, okay?" Dad said. I was quiet but curious. I think Quin and Aaron went on to ask the questions that I didn't have the words to ask. "Why can't we stay at Mom's house? Why can't we stay at your house?" they asked. Still crying, my dad answered their questions as best he could. He told us how he and my mom were sick and that we'd be staying with our cousin Whitney and her son Anthony until they could get some things sorted out. I remember him apologizing, saying that he and Mom had fucked up, and then excusing his language. He asked us if we knew how much he loved us. I grinned and said yes. I'd developed a habit of smiling or laughing when I was in an uncomfortable situation.

The rest of our dad's talk was him telling us about this lady, who turned out to be our social worker. I'll never forget her name — Kristin Mason. She chimed in every so often while my dad was talking, explaining her role as our worker.

I wondered if she had black in her because her complexion was light but not pale. For the next while, my dad was quiet as Kristin explained how this was all temporary. "Six months, tops! Mom and Dad are going to be getting some help so they can be better for you guys," Kristin said.

The transition from Mom's house to Whitney's wasn't too bad. We all crowded into her apartment along with her and her son, Anthony. We'd already grown up around her, living in Mulgrave Park, so at least she wasn't someone *entirely* new to us. However, it was new to her because she went from having one child to having four children in a three-bedroom apartment. It worked out for a few months; things were pretty normal, given the circumstances. She treated us like the family that we were. Once we'd established a routine, she allowed us to venture back to my mom's neighbourhood, on the bus, to hang out with our friends. I missed Nikko all the time and I went to see him as much as I could. He even inspired my very first poem, titled "When I Dream." It went something like this:

When I dream, I dream so special
I dream of things so true
I find the best time to dream, is when I dream of you
I look towards the future, to find what it will be
And when I do, I smile because this is what I see
I see myself holding you tight, throughout the day and
through the night

One boring day, I was surfing the internet at Whitney's house and stumbled upon a poetry contest where the prize was publication in a book, receiving a free copy and earning fifty dollars. I entered the poem I'd written about Nikko and to my surprise, I won!

It felt good seeing my work amongst the thousands of other poets who had entered the contest from across Canada. Writing became my thing. It was nice to have something that was mine. Meghan, who was sixteen years old at the time, was told by the social worker that she was old enough to make her own decision and she had chosen to stay with our mom. Since I didn't have Meghan to talk to anymore, I decided to start a diary. I wrote about Nikko and complained about how much my siblings got on my nerves. I often daydreamed about what life would be like when I got older and had a family of my own. I must've come up with a thousand baby names before I tired and started a new journal book.

Eventually, the four of us children became too much for my cousin. We all fought more often than not and believed that Anthony got away with everything because he was the youngest. Halfway through the first semester of grade six, Kristin came to have another meeting with us and told us that Quin and I would be moving to Spryfield. We were entering the foster care system.

The first thing I noticed about our new foster mother was the spots on her face and arms. They didn't look like freckles or pimple scars. She was a black lady and she had dark marks all over her face and arms. I wondered and wondered what they were from. They looked scary. She seemed friendly enough, but Quin and I were miserable about having to move.

I didn't talk much. We were so far from everything that we knew, living in a hood that wasn't our own; so far that we had to get up at 6 a.m. every day so that we could make it to school on time for 9 a.m. Over the course of a few months, we developed a routine there at our new foster mother's house. Her name was Audrie and she had a spoiled rotten daughter named Raina. Our routine consisted of a 6 a.m. rising where we would shower, get dressed, attempt to brush our hair into something that resembled a ponytail, eat and wait for our driver, Kim, to take us to school. Kim was the real deal: a cool white girl who played all of the hood music that we used to listen to before Audrie's house rules were imposed on us. Kim drove a small, silver Neon. She always drove with one hand on the steering wheel and one foot propped up on the door. Quin and I loved her and we often fought about who would ride up front with her. Every time Kim parked outside to wait for us to get out of school, I could hear her bumping music artists like Usher and Lil Wayne. Kim had this way of dealing with us that never felt like she was being bossy or rude, unlike other drivers that we would encounter over the long years of being chauffeured back and forth to school and weekend visits with our parents.

I tried hard that year in school. It was my last year of elementary at St. Joseph's A. McKay. All of my old girl friends were still there and Amir and Raury were there too. When I came to school on the first day, decked out in a pink jogging suit with matching, pink, high-top "Fresh" sneakers, I thought I was too cool. Unfortunately, the sneakers that I'd been so hype about turned out to be imitation Phat Farm sneakers. At that time, I knew nothing about imitation anything. I guess I was the only one, because a few kids teased me all day. I was so embarrassed. After that, I refused to wear my pink high tops or anything else that was imitation.

At lunch time, I quietly walked up the street to my new babysitter's, along with Aaron who was in the fifth grade at this time. We weren't like some of the kids who could afford to buy fast food every day so we were forced to go to this lady's house for dreadful lunch after dreadful lunch, an arrangement made by our social worker.

Mrs. Thomas was a sweetheart, but a sweetheart who knew nothing about expanding her food palate. *Every single day* for an entire school year, we ate Kraft Dinner. On Fridays, we would get bread and wieners to add to the guck — if we were lucky! Eventually, we learned to spice it up with salt, pepper, sugar or ketchup. Some days when Aaron felt like acting up, he would kick me under the table and make gagging noises at the food and we'd laugh until Mrs. Thomas came in and told us to be quiet. Other days, I would show up at the house alone and Mrs. Thomas would ask me where Aaron was. I always said I didn't know, but of course I did. He had run off with his friends to share a slice of pizza or a burger from Burger King.

Mrs. Thomas had a granddaughter who would eat with us sometimes. She was a beautiful little girl, a few years younger than Aaron. She had another type of good hair that you could wet and twirl around in your finger to make it curl. I remember times when I'd find her copying my actions at the kitchen table. She would chew when I chewed, put her spoon down when I did and ask to put salt on her Kraft Dinner, claiming she needed it. It was annoying at the time but kind of sweet too.

The school year dragged on and soon it was winter. That year, we'd had one of the worst winters that Nova Scotia had ever seen. "White Juan," the meteorologists on TV had called it. The snow was higher than my waist. For a day or two, we were snowed in at Audrie's house in Spryfield. We were bored out of our minds. When we finally did get plowed out of our little prison, we couldn't help but get a little crazy. What started out as us shoveling Audrie's car out turned into a snowball fight between us girls. It was Audrie's daughter Raina versus Quin and me. Without so much as a head's up, Quin threw a well-packed snowball *straight* into Raina's face! We could hear the impact from where we knelt behind a huge snow bank. The little girl let out a loud wail and her wet, snowy mitten went immediately to the centre of her face.

Even though Quin had been the one to hit Raina with the snowball, her mother had *me* shipped out as well, without a moment's hesitation! Although I wasn't fond of Audrie, no more than I was that awful Kraft Dinner at Mrs. Thomas's house, I couldn't help but ask the question as we drove off to what I thought was our new home. "How come I have to move too if it wasn't me?"

We're almost teenagers. Who would want us? I thought. Then, instead of housing us together, they sent Quin to a group home in another part of the city.

I was reluctant during the drive to my new house, where my new foster parents were met with a grim look. "This is only temporary," Kristin informed me. "Thirty days tops until we can find you another place to live," she'd said. She went on to explain the details of my accommodation there. Luckily for me, I had my own room. Two other kids, both adopted by my new foster parents, lived there as well and were near my age, so it didn't feel so bad. My foster mother, Marie, was an older, potbellied lady who dyed her hair from gray to ginger red. Marie stayed in a pair of heels. Not the stiletto kind but the comfy ones that told you she was a mom. Her husband, Daniel, was enormous with a thick, kinky beard, a mustache that covered his top lip and large sausage-like fingers.

Marie and Daniel turned out to be quite the pair. I could tell they were firm but not strict by the way they spoke. They were also very gentle and relaxed. Marie was a true caregiver. Each morning and every lunch hour, she asked me what I wanted to eat. It was a big difference from my mandatory consumption of Kraft Dinner the previous year. Often, she would give me five dollars for lunch so that I could go to McDonald's with my friends — a posse that included Nikko, my old graffiti drawing, boob-grabbing love. One Tuesday, I came home and asked Marie for money to go to KFC for Toonie Tuesday (back when it *actually* cost you two bucks). She gave me a five and when I told her I didn't need that much money, I was rewarded with being allowed to keep the entire bill for being honest. In those days, you felt like a boss if you were able to say, "Lunch on me!" to one of your friends. So that day, I told one of my girls to hustle the change to cover the tax and I would pay for the rest. We ate fried chicken and French fries and drank root beer like we owned the place!

Daniel was a hearty man, the type of guy to tell a sarcastic, slightly funny joke at the dinner table. "Let's hear it Jade. What did you learn today?" he'd say. This was our typical topic of discussion at dinner. Usually I would say that I hadn't learned anything but occasionally I'd reel off a random math equation that I only half understood. When my poor response didn't suffice, he'd ask me what I was thankful for. In those moments, I'd swiftly name my friends and family. "All right, Matt, let's hear it. You're next," Daniel said. Matt was their adopted son.

Matt was the youngest in the house. Naturally, I thought he was spoiled. He was a reserved type of guy. Unlike me and Tara, he got away with quick, mumbled responses.

He was always sarcastic. From what I gathered about his birth mother, she died young from some type of health problem that caused her heart to give out. I think it was Marie who once said she'd died from a broken heart. If you were looking for Matt, you could usually find him in the living room playing *Call of Duty*, in the kitchen eating or in the dining room huffing and puffing over his homework that his parents were forcing him to complete. Tara, their adopted daughter, was another story. She argued a lot with Marie and Daniel and she was often told to go to her room. "Why is she always so mad?" I asked Marie once. "Tara has attachment issues," Marie replied. I didn't know what she meant so I dropped the subject. Just as I was getting comfortable there, the thirty days were up. This time, instead of a new set of foster parents, I was sent to a group home called Sullivan House. It was close enough that I could go to the same school. I was also close enough to walk back to Marie and Daniel's house, but I never did. I didn't last long at the group home — that placement was also temporary.

Over the next year or so, it was a series of moves for me. I barely had anything, so I mostly lived out of a few bags. Even when I had the chance to unpack, I always made sure to be able to repack quickly in case of a short-notice move. The second group home I went to, the Reigh Allen Centre, felt like jail. I've never been arrested but the way the rules were set up, I imagined it was very close to what it felt like to be on twenty-four-hour lockdown. When I first got there, on a Friday, it was mandatory for new intakes to stay inside for forty-eight hours. I nearly lost my mind. I had no contact with the outside world. No cellphone. No computer. No friends on the inside. No visitors allowed. When I was finally allowed out, Quin managed to come visit me.

I was free for a few hours at least. I jumped into her arms and happy tears sprang from my eyes.

My only other experience with happy tears, in that period of my life, was when I got the news that I was granted permission to leave the group home and live with my Uncle Viez and his wife, CiCi. In my mind, I thought that because I was with family I'd have to adhere to fewer rules. I was very wrong. My aunt and uncle were an older couple with strict rules. My curfew was embarrassing and I wasn't allowed to hang out on Creighton Street where all of my old friends lived. It was a nightmare. The only plus side of the whole ordeal was that I had a king-sized bed and a computer in my room. If you were looking for me in the house, you could usually find me in my room, on the ancient messenger platform, MSN. Sometimes, my little cousin Leah and I would pull up our favourite songs on YouTube and sing our hearts out. "Shoulda Known Better" by Monica was our theme song, even though at that time I didn't really understand the way she felt insulted by her boyfriend's lack of trust in her while he was incarcerated.

As with every other place, eventually I had to move. Apparently, my aunt and uncle didn't like my attitude. Moving was exhausting. Somewhere between foster parents that didn't want me and group homes that couldn't house me, I changed social workers. Kristin, my first social worker, was for temporary foster kids only. Our new worker, Geanne McNeil, was for kids in permanent care, which I was now in, along with Quin and Aaron. This meant that my parents had failed to do whatever it was that they were supposed to do in order to get us back in their care. In reality, we were still their children, but to the system and in society, each of us was now a "ward of the court." The system was our legal guardian. I went back to live at Marie and Daniel's house.

Although I had always been a good kid and a straight-A student, it seemed like none of that mattered anymore. I was hurting and I missed living with my family. I just didn't give a fuck anymore. After the realization that going back to my real family was not possible, I was angry and I was out to show the world just how angry I was. And as far as my self-image went, things got suddenly worse.

I used to have a body made up of beautiful brown skin. Then my body began to attack me from the inside out. What started as that one lump on my bikini line turned into the first of many "flare ups" of painful problems with my skin. I was scared and embarrassed. The medication that the doctor first prescribed me didn't seem to be working because soon I found myself examining lumps under my arms as well. These were more painful than the first set. What started as small, hard lumps (sort of like an under the skin pimple) turned into bigger, pus-filled lesions, which would become so inflamed that they would break my skin and force me to wear gauze bandages for weeks, sometimes months. After the umpteenth doctor's appointment, I was referred to a dermatologist.

I waited impatiently, alone, in the waiting room until my name was called. About a half an hour later, I was led into a doctor's office and given a hospital gown to put on. I was told to sit on the table until the doctor came in. A few minutes later, as my eyes gazed over the diplomas posted on the wall, a man came into the room. I sighed heavily. He told me to show him the problem areas and I had to muster up the courage to show my private parts to a male doctor I'd never met before. I was embarrassed but I wanted help. I wanted the pain to go away. He asked me if there were any other areas with the same problems and tears filled my eyes. Though it wasn't as bad as my bikini area or underarms, there was another problem area — my butt. He asked if he could take a look so I bent over, using my hands to help him see more clearly. My self-consciousness disappeared in a blanket of shame. I heard him say, "Hmm," before giving me the go ahead to put my clothes back on as he left the room for a moment.

The doctor returned with a small package of papers and a prescription notepad. Feeling sick to my stomach, I folded my hands across my lap as he began to speak. I only half listened to him as he drew a small diagram and told me something about my apocrine glands, which is where sweat is produced. He prescribed me an antibacterial soap, a lotion to put on my skin and another round of antibiotics. He handed me the papers as well and told me to make an appointment with the secretary to come back in six months. I took the papers and decided to wait until I got home to read them.

When I got home, the words "Hidradenitis Suppurativa" were written across the top of the paper. I had no idea how to pronounce the words so I tried to sound them out over and over: "hi-dra-den-i-tis sup-pur-a-ti-va." *What the fuck does that mean?* I asked myself. I held the papers with a blank look on my face. A skin disease. The words repeated themselves in my head until I'd built up a silent rage. I burst into tears. I was so confused. *How the hell did I get a skin disease?* I thought. I flipped through the pages again until I got to the "Causes" section. A few theories were listed but it said that the cause is ultimately unknown. I wiped my tears and went to the "Description" section again.

Going over the text a second time revealed my worst nightmare. There is no cure for Hidradenitis Suppurativa.

A million questions ran through my mind as I threw the papers on the floor and sobbed into my pillow. I cried until I fell asleep. It was the beginning of a decade-long depression that the world knew nothing about. Some days were better than others. Sometimes I'd see weeks of remission, only to wake up and discover a new outbreak. I had dark scars in all of my problem areas (underarms, groin and butt).

Tank tops became a thing of the past. On too many occasions, I had to throw out my t-shirts because they had yellow and red stains on the underarms from pus and blood. I never wore white panties anymore or used white towels. I had to wash my sheets and pillowcases quite often because of leakage. Following doctor's orders, many nights I slept in the most uncomfortable positions with hot cloths under each of my arms and one between my legs. I had to buy another pillow so I could sleep with one for my head and one between my legs when the weight of my leg on top of the other one became too painful. I missed school a lot. Too depressed to get out of bed, I hid amongst my covers all day long, only getting up to eat and use the bathroom. Sometimes, I wouldn't even eat. It was easier to feel that hunger ache and listen to the hollow growls of my empty belly than to concentrate on the unbearable pain I had to deal with in order to lift my arms.

At home, alone in my room, I became a nudist. Clothes were too painful to wear. Anything that restricted my movement or caused friction to my problem areas were my worst enemy. I would float in and out of consciousness as I hid in my sleep, the only place I could go to avoid the pain. You don't feel pain while you're asleep. However, a lot of the time I would awaken in agony from trying to lie in the wrong position. It was disgusting. I was living a nightmare. It's ironic that I can sit and watch horror films all day and night with gruesome scenes of blood squirting from murdered bodies and feel nothing, but as soon as I see my own blood pour from one (or all) of my problem areas, my heart races and I feel nauseous. I panic until I realize that it is just another lesion and I am not bleeding to death. There were plenty of times when I sat in the shower or laid in the tub, weeping. It seemed like every inch of my body was in pain. None of the products the dermatologist prescribed were doing me any good. It was just me against the pain.

CHAPTER 3

LOVE AND SEX

Still at Marie and Daniel's house, it was their son who gave me my first orgasm when I was fourteen. Feelings of embarrassment, shame and a pulsing feeling between my legs took too long to subside the first time it happened. We'd been sitting on the couch in the living room, watching a movie. His hand casually grazed my foot, then my leg. I thought he was just adjusting his sitting position so I moved a bit to get out of his way. His hand touched me again. This time it got closer to my thigh. My heart started racing. *Was he touching me on purpose?* I wondered. I didn't want to look at him — it felt too awkward. I tried to stay perfectly still. I was wearing pajama pants with a string around the waistband. Gradually, the string came undone. My body was tense. Still, I kept my eyes straight ahead, toward the TV. Before I knew it, his hand was inside my pants, touching the top of my vagina. He moved his fingers in a circular motion until I felt a pulsating sensation there. I'd masturbated before so the feeling was familiar, but I'd never had another person make me feel that way. I thought I could hear my heart beating in my ears. *Oh my god, what if someone comes in?* I thought. He quickened his motion until I felt it coming. I was going to orgasm. I held my breath. If I made any noise, someone might hear us. When I let out a low sigh, he stopped and moved his hand away from me. I remained still. It didn't take long for a wet gush to gather in my pants. I couldn't believe what had just happened. I sat there in silence until Marie told us it was time to go to bed. I went downstairs to my room, changing out of my pajama pants that were now wet on the crotch.

As time went on, we developed an unspoken routine. Whenever we found ourselves alone in the living room, his fingers would find my crotch. He grew bolder with time, shoving his hands down my pants when others were sitting with us in the dimly lit room, unknowingly within earshot of a muffled orgasm. Sometimes, I simply wasn't in the mood to be bothered by him and I fought his hand off of me, quietly and aggressively under that damned blanket. Other times, he'd pull my hand until it was in his pants, gripping him tightly. With his hand over mine, he'd stroke himself slowly. I felt disturbed, embarrassed and aroused all at once. He was my foster brother and probably two years younger than me and he was making me orgasm and there was nothing I could do or say to make him stop completely. I didn't even know if I wanted it to stop.

On a road trip to Boston in the spring, we were in the very back seats of his parents' minivan and he was at it again. I couldn't believe his boldness and I wasn't having it in such a small space. I slapped and squeezed his hand until he stopped. When we made a pit stop, I purposely switched seats with my foster sister, Tara. This got me off the hook, for a little while at least. When we finally arrived at the hotel and got settled in for the night, Matt's mouth found my bare feet from where he lay on a cot at the foot of the bed Tara and I were sharing. I'd never had my toes sucked before. It was awful and arousing at the same time. After that, I kept my feet tucked in under the blankets.

One time we almost got caught. We were renting a cottage near Atlantic Playland. Everyone was outside, either in or around the pool. I had ditched them to cool off and went into the cottage to read a book. Matt came in sometime after me, changing from his swim shorts to the pajama pants I was so familiar with, with no boxers. He sat at the opposite end of the couch from me and draped a blanket over both of us, from the waist down. I continued to hold my book in front of my face as if I were reading it. Every so often I'd peer over the top of the pages to see what he was up to. He found my crotch again, only with his feet this time. Using his hands, he directed my feet to either side of his penis, so that they would stroke it. Then he moved my feet to his mouth and began licking the soles of my feet and putting his tongue between each of my toes, even more determined than the night in the hotel. His cheeks grew pink. He pulled my pajama pants until they slid under my bum. Then, he positioned himself so that his face was between my legs. I sat there, frozen in shock, book still in hand, trying to process what was happening as his tongue licked me hard. I remember the wetness of his saliva. I was squirming and containing my moan as best I could, hanging onto my book for dear life.

Just then, a loud knock came at the door. Quick and calculated, he regained his composure and tied the string on his pants as he walked to the door that he had locked. It was Marie. I focused my attention back on my book in an attempt to hide my flustered cheeks. "Why is the door locked?" she demanded to know. "You're not allowed to lock the door, Matt," was all she said. He gave her his usual muffled, sarcastic response and came back to sit on the couch. Shortly after, Tara and Daniel came in behind her.

Back at the house, my social worker, Geanne was called to talk to me about my behaviour. I was acting out a lot — staying out past curfew, talking back to adults, and getting suspended. "What do you want to do?" she asked me. "I want to go live with my mom," I groaned. This time, going home to my mom was an option. I wasn't quite sixteen yet, which is usually the age where you can decide if you want to live with your parents, but apparently my mom was doing better and so I made the transition back to living with her at her townhouse in Dartmouth.

Quin had also moved back in with our mom and the two of us began hanging out with this feisty, petite, light-skinned girl named Videll. She looked like she was from America, or at least not from Nova Scotia. She didn't dress how most of the other girls dressed. She was beautiful, with long, curly hair. She had an attitude to match mine, which led us to argue a few times, but nothing serious enough to end our friendship. Anytime I was home in Dartmouth, I was usually with Quin and Videll. Videll lived with her parents and three brothers. Videll's mom, Miss Jasmine, was a thick-skinned, shapely white woman. I didn't know who was crazier, Miss Jasmine or my mom. Although Miss Jasmine was nice and treated Quin and I like her daughters, she held her tongue for no one. I'd cringe sometimes when we were told to "go the hell outside" whenever we tried to pile up in her house to avoid the heat. Videll was allowed to have a boyfriend too, so that was cool. From the time I met Videll's brothers, I immediately had a crush on one of them. His name was Zee. It didn't take long for us to begin fooling around. He was the best kisser I'd ever experienced. All of Miss Jasmine's children had huge, full lips. Zee was no exception, although Miss Jasmine was not his biological mother. Zee and Videll shared a father. In my mind, there wasn't any man who was more beautiful than Zee. Sometimes, I'd go to Videll's house just to catch a glimpse of him. It didn't seem to bother Videll or Quin very much. Besides, the three of us became best friends. Sometimes it felt like the two of them didn't want to hang out with me but whenever I said it, they both told me that I was weird. "Come if you're coming," Quin would say when she was getting ready to go to Videll's house and I'd ask why they didn't invite me. "You don't need an invitation. Just come," Videll said.

I also began hanging out with this girl named Tessa from school. I'd seen her around my neighbourhood too but never really interacted with her. A few times, she'd hung out in the girl's bathroom with me, Laila and our friend Jordan, chatting about guys. Tessa was very open. We talked about shaving our vaginas for the first time, which everyone had been doing except for me. I felt left out. I didn't know the other girls had already begun shaving down there. The main topic of discussion as we crowded around the bathroom sinks was guys. I told them about my first time having sex and Tessa showed us the outrageous positions her body was able to bend into during sex. It was always a laugh fest hearing Tessa explain herself. We started hanging out outside of school too. I went to Tessa's house, where she lived with her mom. I called her mom Aunty, out of respect of her being older than me — something my mom had taught me from childhood. "Don't ask me for no more after today," Aunty said to Tessa just before she headed out of the door. Tessa rolled her eyes. "Ask her for what?" I asked. "Weed. She always says that," Tessa said, showing me the gram of weed her mom had just handed her. I'd smoked before with a girl from school but it hadn't been an everyday thing. But whenever I was at Tessa's house, we smoked. "All Mom says is that we have to smoke in the house," Tessa said. I was fine with that because any time I smoked, it was so obvious I was high that I didn't want to go outside anyway. We'd smoke, make snacks, laugh and talk about boys. When we weren't high, we were practising dance routines choreographed by Aunty. We had a dance group that performed a few times at events. Aunty would teach us each part of a routine then retreat to her room, but before leaving she would give us a stern look. "You should have it down pat by the time I come back out here," Aunty said. We usually caught on pretty fast. Whenever we weren't in rotation when Aunty got back, she would accuse us of slacking or being high. Sometimes we were high, but we usually saved it for after practice.

Tessa was really into doing hair and was quite creative when it came to styling. I didn't always like her choice of hairstyle — sometimes, it was too bold for me. I usually just wore my hair in a ponytail or a bun on the top of my head. "Can I braid your hair?" she would ask while bored. She would have my hair braided up into a style within a couple hours. A lot of people told us that we looked alike, especially when we both had our hair braided. We wore the same size clothes too so it wasn't uncommon to see us rocking the same shirt or outfit.

That summer, Tessa insisted on introducing me to "her

brother." I knew she didn't mean her blood brother because I'd met him already and he was older than us, already not living at home. "Who is he?" I asked.

"His name is Jody. He's all that! He's gonna love you, watch," she replied.

"You're so dumb," I said, laughing. Jody was from North Preston but everybody called it Up Home. He was best friends with Tessa's boyfriend. Tessa had invited them to the Buskers, a street performer festival that happened every July on the Halifax Waterfront. It wasn't so much the performances that were interesting as the people. I always went anyway, because it was the spot for people from nearly every hood in the summer, so I agreed to at least meet him.

When I met Jody, I kept my cool. He was a pretty boy. I could immediately see why girls would throw themselves at him. He had beautiful brown eyes and light skin, tanned perfectly from the July sun. He wore his hair in short curls. His size was what really caught my attention. For being fifteen years old, he was big. It wasn't an "I work out" big, but a husky big. "Hello," he said when we approached him. "What's up?" I asked in greeting. "You're some pretty," he replied. I blushed. Tessa stood beside us smiling. She gave him a hug then went to stand off to the side with her boyfriend. Jody said something along the lines of me letting him call me sometime. I didn't have a cellphone so it was easier to say no. "I don't think so," I said. "Why not?" he asked. "I was told not to talk to boys from Up Home," I told him. I was telling him what my mom had told me. She hadn't gone into detail about why it was a bad idea. She just told me to stay away from them. He looked at Tessa with a smirk. "Oh, she don't like me," he said to Tessa. They started laughing and I just smiled.

The four of us (me, Tessa, Jody and Malik, Tessa's boyfriend) began chilling on the regular. The guys would get a drive to Tessa's house from Up Home. Her mom was gone a lot but even when she was home, she didn't mind too much. She would just stay in her room. Whenever Tessa's house got too boring or her mom didn't feel like allowing company to come over, we would go across the street to Malik's uncle's house. Sometimes it was just us or a few of the boys' friends would scatter about the house. Tessa loved disappearing into her room with Malik, leaving me alone with Jody. He continued to try to convince me that he and I should get to know each other, but I held out. On the days when they couldn't come to Halifax, Jody would call me on Tessa's phone. I liked talking to him but I still didn't fully trust him. He was too pretty! He could probably have had any girl he wanted.

I had one up on him until a few weeks later when he cornered me in Tessa's apartment lobby and kissed me. Before that kiss, he obviously liked me more than I liked him, but that kiss changed how I felt. Things escalated pretty quickly after that. I'm not sure when we said "I love you" to each other but it happened. For me, it was natural — the way I felt. Jody was perfect for me. We got along extremely well. I mean, we *never* argued. We enjoyed every minute of being together. Whether we were relaxing in the house or at a party, we were inseparable. The only time I can think of when we weren't so attached to each other is when Black Tournament, the biggest annual basketball tournament in the city, rolled around. I guess he preferred to be with his boys when it came to basketball. I wasn't really into it anymore once I'd stopped playing but the tournament gave us something to do so Tessa and I went, meeting up with a few other girls from our hood.

Soon after Jody's sixteenth birthday where we partied it up, it was Black Tournament time. Everyone was dressed in their best even though it was May and the weather had been pretty gloomy. I threw on a white wife beater with black jogging pants and my black Timberland boots. I didn't care too much about what I looked like, especially not in the rain. When the game was over, we headed outside with everyone else, and this girl named Shana initiated a fight with me in front of what must have been a hundred people. All I really knew about her was that she was dating the younger brother of a girl I knew in the hood. "She's ugly," I'd said at the time when people realized they were dating. Apparently my remarks had reached her somehow because she told me she knew I had called her ugly, then told me to put my hands up. I had been terrified because I never fought before. Luckily, I had apparently inherited my parents' temper and quick hands as a fighter. I knew my siblings could fight but I had always been the timid one. I stood, hesitant, waiting for her to attack me in front of this huge crowd of people. She didn't budge. Someone pushed her into me once, nothing happened. Twice, nothing happened. *If she doesn't try to hit me the third time, I'm just gonna hit her*, I told myself in a pathetic mental pep talk. Third time, nothing happened. *GO!* I screamed inside my head. With all my might, I fed her punch after punch.

Everyone started yelling and cheering us on. I had no idea what I was doing. With each punch I gave her in the face and head, she hit me on either side of my ribcage. We wrestled a bit and I managed to get her against a car. She tried to hit me in my face and ended up scratching me twice on my cheek. I grabbed her with my left hand and gave a clean uppercut to her chin. Again, I heard everyone yelling.

One guy asked loudly, "Oh my god, was that an uppercut?" Feeling the scratches stinging my face, I got even more riled up. My right hand was getting tired so I switched it up. This time, I grabbed her shirt with my right hand and gave her a left hook. She crumpled down to a squatting-fetal position. "Get her! Get her!" the crowd chanted. I gave her a chance to stand. "Get up!" I said to her, panting. She didn't move so I kept on punching her. I had wanted to let her up, but when I thought about why we were fighting to begin with, I got mad at the situation she had put me in. All of this was because I told someone she was ugly. By now, I was jabbing away with both hands.

Suddenly, someone's hands scooped me up under my armpits and dragged me off of her. I thought I was about to get jumped. "Get off me!" I yelled. I kicked and screamed until the crowd was away from me and I was back inside the lobby of the basketball stadium where I had just been watching a game. I turned around, ready to fire at whomever, as soon as my feet were able to touch the ground again. "Miss Jade!" It was my dance teacher from junior high. I was too hyped up to even begin to calm down. "I'm going back out there," I said, breathing heavily. She sat me down. "You're gonna sit right here. You already won. You don't need to do anything else to that poor girl," she said. I sat there until I had calmed down a bit. She didn't let me get up until she checked to make sure the girl was gone.

When I got back outside, I heard a bunch of people saying, "There she is!" I was being praised! "Jade, you fucked that girl up! I didn't know you could fight," they said. "Me either. That was my first fight," I told them. The guy who had broadcast my uppercut punch asked me where I'd learned to hit like that. He cleared a space to demonstrate what I'd done, saying that was his favourite part of the fight. Everyone started laughing. I made my way to leave and those who were going my way continued to hype up the fight the whole way down the street.

Later on that weekend, I saw some Toronto guys reenacting the fight. "Yo fam, you shoulda seen her! She was so pinch! She got mash up!" they said, in their Toronto slang, giving each other props. Tessa and I started laughing. "Why are you laughing? We're serious! Did you see it?" one of them asked, sounding excited. My girl looked at me, smirking and raised her eyebrows as if to ask if I was going to say something. "That was me fighting," I said. They looked at me in disbelief. "Oh shit!" one of them said, giving *me* dap now. "I need to get you a drink!" he said. I gladly accepted and laughed along with them.

* * *

What I loved about Jody was the *feeling* he gave me. That included sex, but it was more than that. Like I said, he was very big for a fifteen to sixteen year old — not fat but not slim either. I always felt safe and protected standing beside him and lying underneath him. He loved to be near me. We were always cuddling or kissing, close to each other in some way. I don't know whether I needed that or just loved it but I cherished it immensely. He provided me with something that I didn't have — intimacy. That's what he gave me.

I felt like I was a priority to Jody, despite the fact that he already had a girlfriend. At first, his having a girlfriend didn't bother me at all. She was out of sight and out of mind. In the time that we were together, most of his attention was on me and I was okay with that. I did think of his girlfriend from time to time but I'd eventually just push it to the back of my mind. I have no idea how he managed to maintain two relationships simultaneously, but he did. She also knew about me. It bothered her, of course, but she dealt with it. It was kind of like that where we were from. Guys saw multiple girls at once. Sometimes the main (first) girlfriend knew about the others and sometimes she didn't. It was largely accepted. I'm still not sure why it was like that. I don't know if my father had multiple girlfriends at one time but it was evident that something had been happening at one point or another because a lot of my siblings are very close in age, if not the same age, and some of us had different mothers. It wasn't that females approved of their man dating other girls but it was something you had to deal with if that was the man you wanted. As long as you were getting what you wanted out of the relationship, I guess that made it okay. I remember nights Jody's other girlfriend would call and he'd either ignore it or pick up and get yelled at. "I know you're with Jade!" she'd say. I would just sit there and watch him try to end the conversation, half feeling bad for her and half wishing that he would hurry up and get off the phone so that he could make love to me again. Once, I'd asked him who he loved more. "I love her because I been with her but I like you more cause you're so cool, man, I love you too," he said. I never knew if that was a good thing or a bad thing so I just dropped the subject.

Our sex was explosive. The first time we had sex was after a party. He stayed over at Tessa's house with me while Tessa's mom was at her boyfriend's house. Tessa disappeared into her room to do her own thing so Jody and I opted for the couch. I told him I needed to shower because I was sweaty from the party and he followed me. My skin condition was in remission, and being under the water with him was heaven to me. The shower was my favourite place to be. We started kissing and soon he was on his knees with the hot water beating down on his back and my hands in his wet, curly hair. There was nothing for me to grab onto and I didn't know what to do with my hands. I moaned his name with tears in my eyes. He held me steady, with ease, until neither of us could wait anymore. We turned the shower off and he took my towel and dried me off, slowly, before we headed back to the living room. He laid on top of me and kissed me. Soon, we were having raw, passionate sex.

Between spending most of my time with Tessa and Jody, at home Marie (who I was living with again) was trying to make sure that I did productive things. We would go on family outings or she would recommend some program for me to enroll in. It was March break when she signed me up for a nursing camp at Dalhousie University. I didn't have much of an interest in nursing but I agreed to go just for the hell of it. The first day was pretty cheesy as they handed each girl in the group a baby-blue Dalhousie t-shirt. We were to wear it for the duration of the camp. The nurses taught us how to administer a needle on a dummy. That part was interesting. I didn't think I could poke a real person with a needle though. The dummy gave me the creeps with its realistic skin texture. The highlight of that week was visiting the unit of the hospital that housed the premature babies. We didn't get to see any of them but they showed us the teeny, tiny preemie diapers and bottles. "Oh my god, they're so cute!" I exclaimed. Everyone agreed.

The high energy of the tour lasted over lunch. I think I sat by myself but I overheard these two girls talking. I was unsure of what they were talking about but I heard a name that was undeniable. They were talking about Malik, Tessa's boyfriend. There wasn't anyone else around the community with that name, so I approached the pair to ask. "Did you just say Malik?" I asked. One of the girls looked at me with a blank stare. I hadn't noticed how pretty she was until she looked directly at me. She stood about nose to nose with me with long, dark brown hair down to her waist. She looked Chinese with a hint of something else, or maybe it was just a tan. I returned my focus to the conversation. "Uhh yeah," she replied. "That's my friend's boyfriend," I told her. She told me that she used to be Malik's girlfriend but now she was dating his other friend. I just *had* to ask her name to be nosey. "Cadence," she replied. I searched in my brain for the relevance of her name. I'd heard it before. Before long, I remembered from where. "Oh! You're Elijah's girlfriend," I said. "How do you know Elijah?" she asked. "I'm Jody's girlfriend. I met Elijah a few times at Malik's uncle's house," I told her. "Jody? That's my brother!" she nearly yelled. I laughed at her energy. "I mean, I take him as my brother. You must be Jade. He told me he was dealing with a girl over Halifax but I told him I didn't know who you were," she replied. We spent the rest of the day sitting near each other at camp. By the end of the week, we talked each other's ears off with gossip about the boys. We exchanged contact info so we could chat over Facebook. I kept her in the loop about everything that went on with me and Jody.

Jody and I continued to see each other, having sex every chance we got. I don't think we used a condom even then. We rarely did. I could probably count on one hand how often we'd used protection. Even when we did, it either broke or he would take it off. I loved how close unprotected sex made me feel to him. I felt like he must have had an enormous amount of trust in me to do that. I wasn't worried about STIs or pregnancy until one day Tessa asked me when I'd last had my period. To my surprise and horror, I couldn't remember. It was nearing the end of June and I couldn't remember the last time I'd bought tampons. Tessa ordered me to take a pregnancy test. Sure enough, it was positive.

I looked at my 120-pound, fifteen-year-old body. I guess, with the skin condition in remission, it was looking lovely and I hadn't been carefully scrutinizing it. I was in disbelief, standing sideways in the mirror. I wondered if my belly was beginning to poke out or if it was my imagination. I had a hint of a belly that looked more bloated than pregnant. I had no symptoms except my lower abdomen was hard. *How had I not noticed this?*

I made my way to Planned Parenthood. It was nearby and my safest bet. I couldn't go to the clinic that I'd been going to my whole life and risk anybody finding out. The doctor at Planned Parenthood did a urine test that confirmed that I was pregnant. She scheduled me for an ultrasound and went over my options. I could (a) go through with the pregnancy, (b) have an abortion or (c) put the child up for adoption. I didn't know what I was going to do but I was a hundred per cent sure that I wouldn't be giving the child up for adoption. That sounded weird and cruel to me. I'd convinced myself that it was a little boy as soon as the pregnancy was confirmed. All I could picture was that child growing up and wondering who I was and why I never wanted him. I decided to speak to Tessa and weigh out my other two options. The doctor told me to try to make my decision quickly because if I was going to have an abortion, I'd need to do so before I was sixteen weeks along. At the time of my ultrasound, I was a couple days past two months pregnant. I thought back to what I was doing two months prior to then. It had been Jody's sixteenth birthday weekend . . .

With this new information, I was still in a daze. "I'm pregnant. There's a baby growing in my belly," I said to myself over and over. So many questions ran through my head. "What will Jody think? What will my parents think? How will I raise a baby? Would an abortion hurt? *Should I even tell Jody?*" That last question was answered for me, by Tessa. "If you don't tell him then I will," she said. I felt more relieved than betrayed when she blurted it out to him one day, despite my promise to her that I would tell him.

"Jade, you're pregnant?" he asked shyly. I grinned at him, feeling nervous about the conversation that lay ahead and excited about how beautiful our child would be if I went through with having him. I nodded my head. He asked to see and touch my belly. I looked away as he did so, hiding my blushing cheeks from Tessa who insisted on expressing her happiness, telling us how cute our baby would be and how we'd better hope it didn't come out with a big head like Jody's. We all laughed.

"Are you going to keep it?" asked Malik. He was the one to bring us all back to reality. His reserved attitude only allowed him to speak when he deemed it necessary to do so. I told them that I didn't know because at that point I truly didn't. Tessa and Malik walked away to give Jody and I some time to talk, alone. He told me that he supported my decision with whatever I wanted to do. I told him I would have to think about it. Before we left to go home, he knelt down to kiss my belly and said goodbye to the baby and me separately. I blushed all the way home, still trying to collect my thoughts.

I went home and started writing. Truth be told, I didn't

feel strongly one way or the other. I wasn't totally into the whole 'being a mom' thing but I wasn't against it either, nor was I totally against having an abortion. In my journal, I wrote about being pregnant. I wrote, *So, I have sex. So what? It's not a big deal.* I talked to Videll about being pregnant. I needed more opinions. This was a hard pill for me to swallow. Videll was her usual self, telling me that I'd be so cute with a little belly. I don't know if she understood how serious it was. I messaged Cadence on Facebook to see what she thought. With as much as we talked about everything else, I knew she would have some good advice for me. "Do you want to keep it?" Cadence asked. "I honestly don't know. It doesn't really feel real," I told her. "Well, Jody needs to step up to the plate and be a man if you're gonna keep it," she said.

A few days later, in the heat of an argument with Meghan, my secret was out. Turns out she had read my journal. "I'm telling Mom you're pregnant!" she said. She went to my mom's room with my journal in her hand. I sat on my bed, waiting for the shit to hit the fan. I was terrified out of my mind. It was about to get ugly, real quick. My mom didn't even know I was having sex, let alone pregnant. I remember thinking that it was every mother's worst nightmare, finding out your baby girl isn't a virgin *and* that she's pregnant, at the same time. Before long, I heard my mom call me. I took a deep breath and went to her room and stood in the doorway.

"So what, *you're having sex and it's not that big of a deal?*" my mom asked, quoting me from my journal. "Yeah," I replied. "And you're pregnant?" she asked. Again, I said yeah. "Come here, I can't hear you! Are you pregnant?" she yelled. I walked closer to her, stood by the foot of her bed and covered my mouth to hide my smile — the same one that I get when I'm in an uncomfortable situation. She thought I thought it was funny. "Yeah," I said. She hollered, "WHO THE FUCK IS THE FATHER?" I said Jody's name quietly. She was standing up now, and got right in my face. Her eyes were bulging out of her head and I was so afraid of what she might do that I started giggling. "DO YOU FUCKING THINK THIS IS FUNNY? YOU'RE FIFTEEN FUCKING YEARS OLD!" she said like a drill sergeant. Before I could respond, she slapped me clean across the face with her opposite hand. The slap was so firm that I fell back into the wall. My mom pushed my face against it instead of her pulling her hand back. When she turned to go back to sit on her bed, I put my hand on my face. *That wasn't so bad*, I thought. "Now get the fuck out of my face and go the fuck in your room 'til I say you can come out. And don't think I'm not telling your father because I am. AND YOU WILL BE HAVING AN ABORTION!" she screamed.

I went to my room as I was told. I sat down on my bed again and took a deep breath. Then, I laughed. This time, I said it aloud — "That wasn't so bad." Still, I was worried about what my dad would say. He was just as crazy as my mom, if not more. He and I weren't very close at that time but we were pretty cool and he was still my dad. He had just come home from jail after doing a two-year bid. I tried to prepare myself for my dad's wrath but I didn't have much time, because my mom called me back into her room, with my dad on the phone.

To my surprise, my dad was calm and collected. He asked me questions and gave me permission to take the phone and leave the room when he heard how quiet I was being in the presence of my mom. I walked downstairs.

"So you're pregnant are ya?" he asked. "Yeah," I replied. "Who's the father? Where's he from?" he asked. "My boyfriend, Jody. He's from Up Home," I said. My dad knew that was another name for North Preston. He sounded so disappointed. "Boyfriend? I didn't know you had a boyfriend, Jadey. Do you love him?" he asked. "Yeah, I do, Dad." With those words, I started crying again. "How do you know you love him? What do you love about him?" he asked. "I just do," I told him. "So, he wasn't using protection?" I grinned, embarrassed at the thought of the picture this was painting for my father. "No," I said. "Well, Jadey. Didn't you know you could get pregnant?" he asked. I cried and stuttered my response, "I made a mistake, Dad."

My dad stuttered too when he replied. I'd always found his stutter to be funny and cute but this time it sounded different. He told me he was disappointed.

"It's okay that you made a mistake but it's a mistake that you can't make again. I don't think you're ready to be a mother yet, Jadey. You're only fifteen years old. That will be very hard, going to school and trying to raise a kid," he explained.

When he asked me if I wanted to keep it, I told him I didn't know but Mom said I had to have an abortion.

"Well, Jadey, I think that would be the best thing for you right now," he said. Before we got off the phone, he forbade me to see Jody anymore and told me that he loved me whether I decided to keep the baby or not.

Meanwhile, Jody was talking to his parents too — his mom in particular. He didn't get in as much trouble as I did because he was very close with her. Despite my dad's instructions, I still saw Jody. One day, his mom asked to speak to me on the phone. She was very polite and she spoke to me in a motherly tone. She admitted that she thought Jody and I were too young, since we were both still in high school.

"I know you two love each other," she said. Like Jody and my dad, she said that she supported my decision either way and would do her best to help me out if I chose to go through with the pregnancy. "You take care now, honey, and make sure you tell Jody to let me know what you decide to do," she said. I recounted the conversation to Cadence. "His mom is really nice. I'm glad she is being supportive. You know whatever you decide to do, I'm here for you if you need to talk," she said.

I still wasn't sure what I wanted to do but my mom was insistent upon me having an abortion, so I let her make the decision for me. "I'm not gonna keep it, Cadence," I said in our Facebook chat. "Are you sure?" she asked. "Yeah. My mom really doesn't want me to keep it and I'm kind of indifferent to the whole thing. I am a little bit sad though," I admitted. "Boo, just think of it this way, you're young, you're still in school. Maybe this will be for the best and everything happens for a reason, you know?" she replied. I felt like she was right.

When it came time for the doctor's appointments, ultrasound and actual abortion, I was glad to have my mom with me. It wasn't something I would have wanted to go through alone. The morning of my second ultrasound, I was told to sit in the waiting room and drink lots of water so that the tech would be able to see properly. I drank until I was sick, literally. My mouth began to water and I held my cup under my mouth. Tears sprang to my eyes at the moment that my mom and I made eye contact.

"Are you going to get sick?" she asked.

I shrugged my shoulders because I wasn't familiar with the feeling of throwing up. An instant later, I power puked *all over* the waiting room. It just kept coming out. As quickly as she could, my mom pulled me into the bathroom where the puking continued. By the time I made it to an empty stall, I had puked on the bathroom door and then it was over. I looked at my mom, wide-eyed and embarrassed of the mess I had just made. I was so exhausted, I burst into tears. My throat hurt.

Despite my puke fest, the tech was able to get a clear picture. I asked if she could rotate the computer screen so that I could see what she saw.

"Sorry but we don't recommend that the patient view the ultrasound when having an abortion," she said.

My abortion was scheduled for the next week. The appointment fell on a Wednesday. Just enough time for my mom to let all of her friends know (in other words, our whole neighbourhood). In the meantime, I was questioned and ridiculed. I was humiliated and exhausted. I just wanted it to be over. One girl approached me and told me that she had had an abortion before and it was extremely painful. A couple of other girls joined the conversation and told me the horrible details of how they "scrape" the baby out of you.

The morning of the abortion, I was not myself. I went through the motions of getting showered and dressed and drove silently beside my mom to the hospital, in a taxi. I was still out of it when the nurse took my blood pressure and listened to my heart rate, going over the abortion procedure. I looked at her blankly.

"Your heart rate is extremely slow. Are you okay? Do you understand the procedure that is about to take place? Is someone forcing you to do this? You know forcing someone to get an abortion is illegal?" she asked.

I only remember telling her, flatly, that I was not being forced. At first, I was the only one there but within an hour about five other girls surrounded me. I wondered what the circumstances of each young woman was. None of us looked at each other. *Five other babies are dying today*, I thought.

When my name was called, I walked into the surgery room quietly. I was in and out of there in no more than ten minutes. The abortion itself wasn't painful but it was extremely uncomfortable. It felt exactly like what it was — like my insides were being sucked out of me. I wondered if my belly was ripping on the outside because that's how it felt on the inside. I didn't want to look. I just lay there.

Afterward, I had to lie in the recovery room for almost an hour to make sure my bleeding was normal. I was pushed out to a waiting taxi, in a wheelchair, by my mom. She helped me into the taxi. I was afraid to move too quickly because my belly hurt.

"What happened?" the cab driver asked.

I expected my mom to go off on him but all she said was, "Oh, just a little day surgery," and gave him our address.

It wasn't the pregnancy or the abortion that saw the end of my and Jody's relationship. It was my realization that I would never have him to myself. Although I *felt* like I was a priority to him, I knew that I would never be his only girlfriend. Instead of sticking around to attempt to earn that title, I told Jody that I would rather end it. He was upset about me leaving but apologized for having made me feel that way.

"Can we still be friends?" he asked.

"Yeah," I said.

We got off the phone and I allowed myself to cry but I knew I made the right decision and was sure that we really would remain friends.

Without Jody tying us together anymore, I slowly fell back from hanging out with Tessa. Besides, she was always with Malik. I resorted to hanging out at the community YMCA where I used to play basketball. They had a teen centre there with a pool table, game consoles, foosball and computers. It was there that I started hanging out with Daneen consistently. She had played the low post position on my basketball team, so we'd interacted and hung out before then, but I was usually with my other friends. Daneen stood at six feet tall and wore glasses that she was constantly pushing up the bridge of her nose, with eyes that always squinted when she was trying to see something far away. Daneen was a little rough around the edges. That aspect of her scared me because she had a bad temper and was almost a foot taller than me, but she was a really cool girl and she looked out for me. We formed a new squad with a couple of other girls but it was usually her and I, attached at the hip. Daneen was that girl who was popular among the guys — not because she was a freak or a slut or any of those things that other females so readily label a girl when she prefers to hang out with the guys. She was a tomboy so I guess she just related to boys. Anyway, Daneen had lots of guy friends and she was always texting one or more of them.

"Give me someone to text, I'm bored," I said to Daneen one night. Some of the guys she texted were from our hood but I didn't want to talk to any of them so she gave me the number of this guy named Carma who played for the North Preston Bulls basketball team. I didn't know much about him except that he played ball and Daneen referred to him as her best friend. In those days, she had multiple guy best friends so I didn't really pay too much attention to that. I think she sent him a quick text letting him know that her girl wanted his number. He agreed and we began texting.

CHAPTER 4
DESTINY

Carma and I were both getting close to our sixteenth birthdays, which were a month apart. Sometimes I would tease him about how I was older than him, telling him to respect his elders. I went to Citadel High School in Halifax and he went to Cole Harbour High School in Dartmouth. We texted or called each other nearly every day. We talked about anything and everything. I told him about the years I'd spent in foster care, living with strangers. I told him about this one foster family in Dartmouth that had three annoying children who I never got along with at all. The more details I revealed to him, he realized that he knew the lady I was talking about. It turned out that the foster siblings I had there were his actual siblings — they shared a dad. Sharing a dad wasn't out of the ordinary to me because my dad has children by other women, but realizing that his mom had been cheated on too made me feel unsettled. I rolled my eyes at how small Nova Scotia was.

It wasn't long before I knew I wanted to be Carma's girl. In my phone, his name went from "Carma" to "My Superstar" after seeing a video clip of him performing a song that he wrote for a music event held in Halifax. Carma dabbled in music. He rapped and had a pretty good singing voice too. His name stayed in my phone as "My Superstar" until the first day I hung out with him and he brought his friend Jaylin. He'd asked to see my phone. I agreed, unbothered by his request.

"Who's your superstar? Me?" he asked, laughing and showing Jaylin, who also laughed. When I told him that it was him, he said, "What? I belong to you?"

I blushed, embarrassed. "Ain't you mine?" I asked.

"No. I belong to my mother," he laughed.

I laughed more out of embarrassment than amusement as we pulled up to McDonald's drive through and he asked me to pay for their food — which I did.

Time went on and Carma and I talked more and more, still not seeing each other very often. His main excuse was that neither his dad nor brother would let him borrow their cars. Finally, he came to visit me at my mom's house. Only Meghan and I were home. I introduced the two and my sister told him that he looked like Chris Brown. I caught him looking at her butt as she walked away.

As Meghan made her way upstairs, Carma and I took over my mom's room, in the basement. We started kissing each other and soon after, he dropped his jogging pants onto the floor. We had sex, and it lasted maybe thirty minutes. It wasn't physically sensual, but in my mind, it was amazing and everything I needed. He didn't use a condom, which made me feel even more connected to him because I thought that meant that he trusted me. I was on birth control at that time — Mom's orders. Once he finished, he immediately said that he had to go. I didn't want him to but he said he had to return his dad's car. He kissed me goodbye and I went back into my mom's room and flopped backward onto the bed, still needing to catch my breath. I felt like I was in love.

Carma and I got closer and closer. I'd never been on a date until I met him. On our first date, as we waited for our food to arrive, he said something I've never been able to forget. "Why are you sitting like that?" he asked.

I felt my face get hot and my whole body tensed up. I was immediately self-conscious, a look of puzzlement on my face. "Like what?" I asked.

"All slouched over like that. Sit up straight when you're out with me. That looks bad," he said, as he demonstrated how I had been sitting versus how I should be sitting.

I apologized to him, looking down at my plate. For the rest of the evening, I made a conscious effort to sit with my back straight and my shoulders squared, facing forward, even though it caused them to ache.

After the time I paid for the food from McDonald's, whenever we went out on a date, Carma picked up the bill. He rarely asked me for money even when I had it. He sold weed, so he always had cash on hand.

We often ate out at a few of our favourite Chinese restaurants. In the wintertime, our favourite date was to Tim Hortons. It wasn't fancy or expensive but it gave us a chance to talk. We always ordered hot chocolate and Dutchie doughnuts. We would sit there talking for an hour or so before finishing. He always made sure I ate. Once I started staying over at his house, where he lived with his parents and older brother, it became a joke amongst us that I 'never refused a good meal.'

Whether it was food, a good morning text or a drive around the city when I needed to escape my own thoughts or get away from my family, Carma took care of it. "I got you," is what he always said to me. Whenever I needed him, he was there. If not physically, then we'd be on the phone and he'd say all the words I needed to hear in order to feel better.

I had long since been ending the texts I sent him with things like *Okay love xoxo* and *Goodnight my love*. One day, on my way to school, we were giving each other our usual well wishes for the day — hoping the other had a good day at school and whatnot. And he just texted the word *love*. I couldn't believe it! *FINALLY*, I thought. I even went as far as asking him if that text was intended for me and he said yes.

"But how do you know? You've never said it before," I said.

"I just know. I wanted to say it on my own time, not just because you said it," he said.

Immediately, I was filled with a sense of belonging — a connection. *So he does love me*, I said to myself. I was giddy for the rest of the day.

With that declaration, I felt both happy and insecure. I became even more self-conscious, wanting to be perfect in his eyes. I finally had his love and I wanted to keep it. As happy as I was, that didn't change the fact that I had a skin disease. It was all I could think about, because at that time I was having flare ups and it was making me feel pretty horrible. Not only was it uncomfortable and painful, it looked gross. Because there was nothing I could do to hide it like I had done in my mother's dark, basement bedroom, I decided to tell him about it while we were texting. It took a lot of courage and him prompting me to "just tell him."

I texted: *I have to tell you something.*
Okay, so tell me.
I told him I didn't know how to say it. *I've never told anyone outside of my family and friends and I hate talking about it because it's gross.*
You're freaking me out. Just tell me.
Ugh, I really don't want to.
He sent me a single text bearing my name and I knew he was getting annoyed with me for dragging it out.
I have these bumps.
He asked where.
On my pie, I replied. Pie was slang for vagina. Realizing that he must be sitting there looking at his phone wondering "*WHAT THE FUCK?!*" I quickly gave him the short version of what I was talking about.
It's a skin disease. It's not contagious but it's rare. It causes me to get bumps on my pie and sometimes I get them on my bum and on my armpits. I've had it for a few years now and they don't know what caused it but there's no way to get rid of it.
Oh, so it's not a STD?
No. I had it before I even had sex.
Oh, so what's the problem?
I was surprised. *You don't care?*
No. That doesn't bother me. It's not something you can help. That's nothing.
The sense of relief that hit me was so strong I had to stop right there in front of the corner store that I was about to walk past. I was so glad that it was over! As much as I didn't want to have that conversation, I was happy that I did. Now I wouldn't have to request the lights to be turned off when we had sex.
We spoke about my skin disease many times after that. He asked me how I dealt with it and if there was anything

he could do to help. I told him about what a nuisance it was to throw t-shirts in the trash because I had a flare up and it would leak on my shirt, staining it with blood and pus, and how I never wore white panties anymore. I'd tried all of the so-called solutions but none of them worked. I continuously told him there was nothing he could do but (him being who he was) he found a way to help me anyway. On multiple occasions when I was having flare ups and we had showered together, he would take my towel and gently dry me off like a mother would do to a child, making sure to pat dry and not rub. He was even gentle when we had sex, careful not to put his weight on my pelvis area when he was on top. He was very sweet to me in that regard. The thing I hated most about my body was not even an issue on his radar. The only thing he hated about it was seeing me in pain, he'd say.

Carma lived with his parents, Mya and Sonnie, and his older brother, Chance. Chance was in and out of the house whenever I was there. Sometimes he'd be in his room or cooking in the kitchen, but he spent a lot of time out with his daughter so we would only talk here and there. Carma's dad was usually at work or tending to something around the house. I didn't interact with him very much. It didn't seem as if any of us did, aside from Mya. The two were married, the same as my parents.

Carma and I crept into the house late one night while his parents slept. On the drive there, I kept asking him if it was okay with his parents that I was staying over.

"I'm bringing you, ain't I?" he asked.

"I ain't tryna get yelled at or kicked out," I said.

I was nervous about meeting his family. What if they didn't like me? It was my first time staying over. In the morning, Carma left me hanging in his room while he went outside to feed the dog. The door was open a crack. I could see the hallway from where I lay on his queen-sized bed. Mya walked past as fast as she'd appeared. I had tried to wave to her but my impulse was too slow and she didn't see my hand.

Carma came back in. "Did you speak to my mother this morning?" he asked.

I cringed. "I tried to but she didn't see me," I replied.

"Mom said you never spoke to her."

"Oh my god! Tell her I'm so sorry," I said.

"Tell her yourself, she wants you in the kitchen," he replied.

I froze for a moment before gathering the courage to leave Carma's room and nervously stepped into the kitchen.

"Hi, how are you?" Mya said.

"Hello, I'm good. How are you?" I asked.

"I'm good. So, what? You couldn't speak?" she asked.

I explained to her what happened.

"Okay. Just make sure it don't happen no more. I don't have no kids in my house that don't speak when they see me," she said.

I apologized and told her it wouldn't happen again. I felt like it was such a cliché way to meet someone's mother for the first time. *Leave it to me*, I thought.

Carma's mom was beautiful and her house was well kept. She faithfully worked full time. *What did she do to deserve being cheated on?* I wondered. She seemed perfect to me, though I know she wasn't because Carma, in telling me about himself, would tell me how he felt neglected when he was younger because his mom was always working. A lot of the time he'd had to fend for himself, finding things to eat. "I ate a whole loaf of bread in one sitting before. That's a damn shame," Carma said. It wasn't that his mom couldn't cook but because she was at work so much, there were a lot of times he went unsupervised. I think he was emphasizing the fact that no one was there to tell him eating an entire loaf of bread by yourself wasn't a good idea.

CHAPTER 5

MONEY AND POWER

More than a year into our relationship, Carma and I were "breaking up" every other week. We argued a lot about the other girls that he was seeing. He claimed they were giving him money and that he didn't care about them how he cared about me.

"I know who my woman is and my mother knows who my woman is so I don't care about what anyone else has to say," he said. Carma was accustomed to the same type of relationships as the one Jody had had with me and his other girlfriend. Because I was the one his mom interacted with and was introduced to as his girlfriend, I was seen as *the* girlfriend. I don't know if other girls were allowed to stay the night or how they were introduced. For me, any other female was just something on the side, as long as Carma and his mom knew that I was his *real* girlfriend. Of course, it wasn't the same for girls. There wouldn't have been a chance that I could have had multiple boyfriends because if I'd said that I had a man, Carma would never have taken me seriously. He very well may have still slept with me or stayed in touch but it was definitely a double standard.

If I ever threw a tantrum and kicked, screamed or cried about it (and the latter, I did), it was no use. I argued that he already had money and that if he would forget about the other girls, he and I could focus on each other and build our money together.

"Talk is cheap," he'd say. "You gotta show me."

What frustrated me most about him interacting with other females — texting them, hanging out with them and taking a couple of them on dates — was that I had to hear about it. We were from a very small place, so secrets were seldom kept and social media only made it worse. At any given time, there were at least two girls posting his name with hearts or telling someone that Carma was their boyfriend. In turn, I would have questions aimed at me like I was on trial. "Jade, isn't that your man?" they would ask me. It was humiliating. Even though it killed me inside to have these girls claiming Carma as theirs, I brushed it off. Besides, everyone knew I was his main girl and that he loved me.

My first summer job allowed me to pull in quite a bit of money. A girl from my old basketball team and I had landed the job through a family connection of hers. We worked as deckhands aboard the *HMCS Sackville* ship on the Halifax Harbour for almost the whole summer. Our duties were split between ship maintenance, acting as tour guides aboard the ship and being cashiers in the gift shop. The maintenance side of it was hard work. We would have to man the ropes, shine the brass, clean the bathrooms as well as sweep and mop the entire ship! Most days it was fun — the two of us would joke around all day and take turns keeping an eye out for our supervisor so the other could have a nap. The job also came with a full sailor outfit, from the corny hat to the black shoes. We made it look cute though. That year, minimum wage was about $7.10 per hour. We scored a little higher than minimum wage and pulled in over $800 every two weeks. As soon as my mom got wind of this, I was forced to give her $300 per paycheque "for rent." It made me furious, but I was still able to have some money for myself and to help Carma out too. I was proud of being able to help him.

He wanted to attend driving school so I agreed to pay half of the amount (probably around $350). I looked at it like an investment. Soon he would have his licence and his dad and brother would have less reason to keep their cars from him and I could see him more! It was a win-win situation.

The time came for him to make the driving school payment so we agreed to meet at the mall so that I could give him the money. After work, I rushed home to change out of my sailor uniform. Meghan was rushing me because she was driving so I never had time to plan out a decent outfit. I threw on an army tank top and a pair of jogging pants and we were out the door.

It didn't take long for me to find him in the crowded mall. When I called him, he was at the top of the escalator by the entrance that we had come in. I was super nervous as the escalator started moving us up to where he stood because he was with his older brother and I knew I looked a mess. I smiled, greeting them and introducing our siblings to each other. I gave him the money; he thanked me and began walking away. I looked after him. My sister looked at me, confusion written all over her face.

"That's it?" she asked.

"I guess so," I said.

We headed back out to her car, me walking with my head lowered, cheeks burning with a shame I didn't understand. Before Meghan and I could leave the vicinity of the mall, I received a text from Carma. Anxiously, I opened it and this is what it said:

Never leave the house looking that bad again. You had me embarrassed in front of my brother. You represent me.

I looked at my phone, speechless. I wanted to tell him that I had been in a rush to get to him but all I could say was, *Sorry.* I made sure to never let that happen again.

When Carma and I weren't arguing about girls and breaking up, we actually spent a lot of time together. These days, if I'm recalling memories with my friend, Videll, she says so plainly that I was 'never around.' I guess I never noticed because I was never around to hear her say that. I enjoyed spending time with Carma. Even though we argued, I preferred to be around him more than my family and apparently more than my friends. But it wasn't just me. He constantly told me he was coming to get me so I could spend a night or two at his house or he would tell me to catch the bus and come to his house. I spent a lot of time on that bus, travelling up to two hours each way. In the beginning, I was terrified to get on that bus because of the notorious reputation that girls from his hood had for fighting. Nothing ever happened to me though.

During my earlier teenage years, it wasn't uncommon for my girl friends and I to drink hard liquor, smoke weed and take ecstasy pills. I was doing all of this before I met Carma and in the first few months that we were getting to know each other. As time went on and we talked about my past more, I began to tell him about (what I thought were) my outrageous and hilarious stories of being drunk and high. He didn't think they were very funny. After we became 'a couple,' though I'm not sure when exactly that was determined, he put a stop to my use of those things.

"I never want to get that call saying something bad happened to you because you were drunk or high," he said.

I was allowed to have a few drinks at a party he'd be attending or if I was with Daneen, whom he knew. It was pretty annoying to not be allowed to get drunk because I was somewhat shy partying without alcohol or drugs. But his reasoning made sense, so I made do. He was just looking out for me. I quit smoking weed cold turkey and it was easier than I thought it would be. He never smoked and I was with him most of the time, so it didn't seem like much of a sacrifice to make for my wellbeing and his peace of mind.

I recall the first time he got drunk while he was with his friends. He insisted on having his friend Devin dial me.

"Jade, Carma is really drunk right now but he keeps saying he wants to talk to you. I'm gonna put him on the phone," Devin said loudly amongst the drunken commotion in the background.

"JADE! These guys got me loaded, man. I love you, ya know! Are you my baby?" Carma said.

I laughed and told him that I loved him too and assured him that I was his baby. His friends were trying to get him off the phone.

"I'M TALKING TO MY WOMAN!" Carma yelled. "Whose woman are you? Tell these guys leave me alone. I'm talking to my woman," he said, his words slurred.

Blushing and covering my smile, I told his friends, over speaker phone, that I was Carma's woman. One of his boys finally got the phone from him and told me that Carma would call me tomorrow. I laughed and hung up, excited to be able to hold this over his head the next day. You know what they say: a drunken mind speaks a sober heart. Surprisingly, he didn't have a hangover the next day but he did say that he wasn't going to get drunk anymore.

"I don't know how people get drunk every weekend. I was out of my senses. I never had no control of myself. I don't like that feeling," he said rather matter-of-factly.

* * *

During the time we spent together, it was like we were always having sex. I'm positive his parents heard us moaning through the vents but they never said anything. On a sunny Sunday, when his mom had her sisters over for a few drinks, Carma and I were in his room fooling around. His room was right off of the kitchen where the company was. We didn't have sex that time but he slid his jeans off and leaned against his bed, smiling and beckoning for me to come to him and give him head. These little games were naughty fun to me. I'd give it all I had, trying to make him moan. He laughed and told me to slow down then he gripped my hair and finished in my mouth. I got up from where I was kneeling, laughing and saying, "I win!" Seeing who could make who orgasm first became our favourite challenge. There were lots of times when we would watch porn in the computer room of his house and turn it into a game of Follow the Leader. We had different preferences for porn but we made it work. After a bit of foreplay, we would have sex right there on the computer chair or kneel down on all fours on the floor. We had sex any time we could and when we couldn't, we'd create the opportunity to do so. We did it all over his room, the basement, his brother's room, outside, in the car, in his parents' room, and if I was on my period, we did it in the shower. I wanted to have sex on his parents' bed but he refused me at first. I asked him why.

"It's disrespectful," he replied.

I was annoyed and insulted, remembering how quick he was to have sex on *my* mother's bed that first time. I was more than happy to remind him of that and he caved in, allotting us only a few minutes. I felt triumphant.

The basement stairs were no exception to our sexual adventures. He'd sit me there and give me head. I'd try to push him away, reminding him that his parents could open the basement door at any moment but he continued, so I allowed him to. When he finished, he hoisted me up against the wall with my legs wrapped around his waist, thrusting into me until I begged him to bring me to the bedroom.

On many occasions when we drove around the city, we'd park up and he would play some old-school R. Kelly. There was no way I could resist him while R. Kelly was telling me that it seemed like I was ready and to give him that honey love! I didn't want to resist Carma anyway. Right there, in the dimly lit parking lot of Point Pleasant Park, we would make love until the windows fogged up and it became hard to breathe. A couple of times, we came out of the car and he would put my hands on the roof of the car and take me from behind or we would walk into the dark park and have sex on a bench or a picnic table. When we did it doggy style on the picnic table, with the cold night air touching me, it nearly set me crazy with ecstasy. On those nights, nothing separated us — we couldn't keep our hands off of each other.

We had a few drinks one night and Carma said he didn't

want to go in the house yet so we drove up the street a bit to his aunt's house, but we never went in. Instead, he pulled the car into her pitch-black driveway until we were hidden from the street's view. We were in plain sight of her house, but it was dark so we went ahead.

"Take your panties off and come out the car," he said.

I laughed and asked him if he was crazy, obeying his instructions. I told him we were going to get caught as I stumbled in the dark to where he stood in front of the car. He kissed me hard and aggressively turned me around, bending me over on the hood and taking me right there in his aunt's driveway.

If there were any sexual limits between us, I don't think we reached them. Although it never happened, we talked about having a threesome with another girl. I wasn't against it but, naturally, I had my rules. We did, however, begin to have anal sex. I detested it when he first asked but he had lube so we went ahead. It took us a few (painful) pokes and awkward positions to get it in but eventually, we got the hang of things. The least painful position was me sitting on his lap to start then we were pretty much free to move around to other positions. The initial pain never went away but once we got going, it felt surprisingly good. I was kind of embarrassed at how much I enjoyed it but my mindset was this: If I say no, there will be another girl who is more than willing to do whatever he wants so I might as well just do it.

He never held my hand in public — in fact, he refused to. Whenever I tried to hold his hand, he would move his arm and either put it around my shoulders or tell me sternly that he didn't hold hands. "Only white people do that," he'd say. It bothered me a lot but I knew I couldn't force him. Instead, we'd hold hands in the car as he drove. But we showed our intimacy in other ways. When we were at his house, we'd take turns cooking breakfast for each other or cook together. I would do the dishes and he would blast music artists such as Charlie Wilson and sing to me and dance around the kitchen. Although he had a pretty decent voice, he made sure to be very dramatic with his kitchen concerts and it would annoy the hell out of me. Still, I laughed when he grabbed my arms and slow danced with me around the kitchen. It was like we were an old married couple with him being annoying and me pretending to hate it but loving every minute of his playful side. Watching him laugh was the best.

He would let me lotion his body sometimes after he got out of the shower and offer to do the same for me. Those mornings, we lived harmoniously — one caring for the other and vice versa. He taught me how to make his bed just how he liked it, with 'hospital corners' like his mom used to do it. He told me exactly where to place his pillows. Eventually, it became habit whenever I slept over. I'd even fold his clean laundry and put it away. Everything had its place — sock drawer, shorts drawer, drawer for undershirts. Dress shirts were put on hangers in the closet, along with jeans and they were only hung right if all of the buttons were done up and the crotch part of the jeans was facing inward. Occasionally, I would clean his sneakers with soap, water, a toothbrush and a rag. I took pride in taking care of those things for him, to be able to know him on those simple terms. Even when I didn't feel like doing it, I would do it anyway because I was happy to lessen his workload. Sometimes, I would write him little notes and leave them in his room or binder or in his jeans pocket. I wrote him a long love letter once but I ended up ripping it to pieces after an argument and leaving it on his bed.

At night, we would cuddle up and watch TV and movies. It was like there was a spot on his arm reserved for my head. Whenever he lay down before me or I'd take a bathroom break, I'd climb into the bed beside him and say, "Let me in." He would open up his arms for me and it was there that I felt the safest. I had a habit of stirring in my sleep, groaning or talking or being startled out of my sleep by a nightmare. He was always right there to console and hold me and tell me it was just a dream. Something a father would do. The odd time when he didn't wake up on nights I nearly jumped out of my sleep, all I had to do was find my spot on his arm again or climb atop him and nestle my head beside his. He'd stir but didn't seem too bothered. He'd ask me what was wrong, I'd tell him I had had a nightmare and he'd kiss and hug me tight. I'd say, "I love you," three times over and the results of the nightmare would turn into a lovemaking session. We also lit candles and had baths together a couple of times.

After hearing a dope verse by Lil' Kim that said, "Everything I do give him the chills, like writing 'I love you' on one hundred dollar bills," I showed him love by doing just that. I figured if he liked money so much then it wasn't a big deal for me to share mine with him. I always made it a point to tell him that money didn't matter to me.

As I said before, Carma and I were "breaking up" every other week. I barely thought of it as a breakup. In my mind, he was still mine and I still belonged to him even when we weren't together. Some days, I was confident of that because we would still converse during the time we were separated. Other days, you would swear we were enemies at war. He even accused me of using him for sex once. I retaliated by saying that all of the stress he caused me wasn't worth using him for sex and that I could have anybody else but I loved him so I wanted to make it work. He went on to tell me how he used to brag to his friends about what a 'good woman' I was and how 'down' I was for him but that he couldn't say that anymore because of how I'd been acting. Being down meant staying loyal and doing whatever it took to keep your man happy. Really, being a good woman meant being submissive regardless of how your man was treating you. If he cheated on you, you were expected to stay with him out of loyalty. I didn't know what I had done to afford such a statement from him but I was convinced that he was right and that I needed to step my game up. His negative perspective of me practically drove me crazy. I would ask if I could stay over at his house and he would tell me that I didn't deserve to sleep in his bed that night but we would see how I acted over the next few days.

It seemed like I was always in some state of confusion, shame or anger. I didn't know what I had or hadn't done but I knew it must have been something because he wouldn't say that just to say it. *It must be true*, I thought. At school one day during a texting war between us, some ugly things were said. I couldn't sit there anymore. I ripped out of the classroom and ran all the way to my mom's house, crying.

"What's wrong?" my mom demanded.

Usually I didn't talk to my mom about my life but I was in such a hysterical state that I yelled, "IT'S CARMA! HE'S DRIVING ME FUCKING CRAZY!"

I shut myself in the bathroom, mad as hell — at myself for being so mad and even madder that I didn't know what I was actually mad about. The argument with Carma had been about everything and nothing at the same time. Our usual fight — I wanted him to myself and he said I had to prove my love. But I didn't know how. I looked at myself in the bathroom mirror with tears streaming down my face and began hyperventilating. My mom must have heard me gasping for air because she came bursting into the bathroom.

"Child, what is wrong?" she demanded, her eyes wild.

"Mom. I. Can't. Breathe," I choked out.

She left me standing there and returned with a glass of water. "If that's how Carma is making you feel then maybe you shouldn't be with him," she said and left me there by myself.

Hearing that, I immediately became angrier, defending him in my mind, knowing full well that I couldn't just *leave* him. I ran myself a bath as hot as I could stand it. I stripped out of my clothes and submerged myself under the water, hair included. I held my breath underwater as long as I could and lay completely still, praying to God and asking him to take me out of my misery. As I came up for air, Meghan slipped into the bathroom.

"Geez, are ya all right, sister?" she asked. Her voice was filled with confusion and concern.

I looked at her out of the corner of my eye and nodded my head. My breathing had slowed to a near stop. I was so exhausted; I wanted to die right then and there. *They just don't understand*, I thought, *I love Carma*.

That fall, Laila and Jordan invited me to attend a group called MAP (Media Arts Program) that was held at one of the universities by an organization called Leave Out Violence, or LOVE. Laila's attendance was mandatory through the courts because she had gotten into some trouble and Jordan raved about the food so I decided to go too. It was a cool group but a lot of the people there were *super* weird. There were emo kids, punk rockers, nerds and a few hood kids. The staff seemed *too* friendly but I liked their vibes so I began to attend regularly.

We wrote and talked about a lot of important subjects

like friendship, feelings, race and education. I was still seeing Carma but we were in limbo again. He and I still did a lot of things we were used to but I felt like I was walking on eggshells. When we talked about healthy relationships at MAP, I felt sad that the ideals we mentioned were not what I was experiencing with Carma. I brushed it off, with arrogance, claiming that that type of relationship only existed in fairytales. I mentioned Carma, my boyfriend, whenever we talked about who we loved and looked up to. I constantly told Carma that he was the smartest person I knew but he tended to scoff at me and ask, "Then how come you never listen to me?" Each time I said, "I do listen."

During one of our MAP sessions, I had a conversation with one of the staff members. His name was Paul and he was a social worker. Paul was a happy-go-lucky type of guy with a shiny, bald head. He was so enthusiastic that I thought he was faking it. *No one can be that happy*, I thought. Either way, he was really nice. He told me that I had leadership abilities and that I could "go to camp" the next year if I continued to display those abilities that he'd seen in me. I had no idea what he was talking about. After hearing me rave about Carma, Paul told me that my boyfriend was a lucky guy and that he'd love to meet him.

I wanted to be friendly so I said, "Maybe," though I already knew that it would never happen. "This isn't really his type of thing," I said to Paul.

Still, he encouraged me to bring him by.

Carma and I continued to go through our cycles of breaking up and getting back together. Around Christmas time, things were shaky so I didn't get him anything because we never discussed exchanging gifts. To my surprise, he had gotten me a present. We sat in his brother's car, near my house where the yellow street lights were glowing on the snow. He pulled out a ring box. My hand shot over my mouth to cover my smile.

"What the hell, Carma!" I said.

He opened the box and there were two rings inside. "This is for you," he said, handing one to me.

I slipped it on my ring finger and it fit perfectly. It was a tiny gold band with a single diamond in the centre. I noticed the other one was much bigger and had a yellow stone in it.

"Who's that one for?" I asked. My immediate thought was that it was being reserved for another woman. I was half right — it was for his mother.

I thanked him repeatedly and felt like shit for not having a gift for him.

"It's cool. I ain't nothing. Carma don't matter," he said with sarcasm dripping from every word.

For the rest of our evening, I felt uneasy and overwhelmed with the ring sitting on my finger. I vowed to never take it off. When I got home, I began to make a plan in my head to get another job so that I could buy him stuff too. I wanted him to know that he was just as deserving of a beautiful gift.

God, I loved that man. He had become everything to me. I shared my whole life with him — the good and the bad. Despite the arguments we had and the times we 'broke up,' he knew just what to do to bring everything back together — to make everything okay again. This time, his magic touch had been a ring. He knew that gold jewellery was my favourite thing in the world!

I held a few jobs while I was in high school, dating Carma. He rarely asked me for money even when I had it. Our dates still came out of his pocket. He always had money. Still, I wanted to do something special for him.

CHAPTER 6
BELONGING

On February 26, 2009, I celebrated my sixteenth birthday. I had all of my friends over for supper and some of Quin's friends came too. My mom was (and still is) the best cook in all of Nova Scotia. She filled the table with a variety of flavours of chicken wings, salads, rice and my favourite — potato salad. Carma showed up as the food was being served. I introduced him to my mom. He kissed her on the cheek and said hello. I was surprised at how composed he was in her presence. Even my longtime girl friends were intimidated by her. I wore purple for him because it was his favourite colour — the LA Lakers were his favourite team.

The winter finally ended and we were still doing okay and getting along. We began to talk about the future. I told him how I wanted to have a family, expressing how much I hated the dysfunction within my own family.

"I don't want to be like that with my family. I feel like it was my mom's job to keep us together and she didn't. So, when I have kids, I'm gonna make sure they're good and they know that I love them," I told him.

He told me how he wanted to flip houses, which I had already suspected because he was always watching those home improvement shows. Somehow, we got on the topic of tattoos. I told him I wanted to get a heart wrapped in barbwire on my arm, similar to the one that Mary J. Blige has.

"It will symbolize how I've had to protect my heart from all the pain I've experienced in my life," I said to him.

"That sounds like a good idea if that's what you want but it sounds sad," Carma replied. "If I ever get a tattoo, I want to get a portrait of Martin Luther King Jr. and Malcolm X," he said. He told me how those were the two men he looked up to the most.

When we talked about what components were missing from our relationship, he said, "You need to trust and believe in me more." I decided that he was right and that 'trust and believe' sounded like a better tattoo than the barbwire heart. He agreed and we started to design it out. I wanted to get it on my lower back but he didn't like that idea because it was too common, so I quickly dismissed it. Since we'd gotten on the topic, I was obsessed with the idea of getting a tattoo.

"You should get my name on you," Carma said. "That will show me that you're for real."

I didn't give much thought to whether it was a good choice or not. *I am for real so why wouldn't I get it?* I thought. I had zero intentions of leaving Carma, ever, and I felt that this would solidify the deal and help him to feel the same.

"Where do you want me to get it?" I asked.

He told me he wanted it right on my thigh. He said he

knew a good artist and I agreed to get it, as long as he paid for it. With that being said, I began to hunt for the perfect font.

Over the next week or so, I spent the entire period of my computer class searching for fonts. There were thousands to choose from. I went through hundreds of samples. Finally, I found it. It was simple but intricate. It was one of those Disney storybook fonts where the first letter was big and fancy. I printed it out in a size that I thought was suitable and took a picture to send to Carma. He loved it! I was so giddy; I went home and showed my mom.

"Mom, I'm gonna get a tattoo, wanna see it?" I asked.

She looked at me without expression when I showed her the sketch.

"What's that say?" she asked.

I traced the C with my finger, showing her how it said Carma. She was in the bathroom, putting her lipstick and eyeliner on to go out. She laughed and said, "You better go sit down somewhere, little girl. You ain't getting that boy's name tattooed on you! Don't be so foolish."

I shrugged her off. "Okay, don't believe me," I said.

"What if you guys break up?" she asked.

I assured her that we wouldn't and she said okay, clearly irritated.

Two weeks later, Carma and I pulled up to the tattoo guy's spot. The man was a crack addict and did a lot of the boys' tattoos from my hood. As he was applying the sketch on my thigh, he said, "Who's Carma, you?" pointing to Carma, who took a moment to look away from his phone and nod his head.

Looking at me now, he asked if I was sure I wanted to do this. "I don't usually do boyfriend tatts. Girls usually regret it and come back for a cover up a few months later," he said.

I told him I was sure and he began tattooing while Carma watched. When he finished, Carma paid the man and we left.

In the car outside the tattoo guy's house, I asked Carma, "What's wrong?" He seemed distracted. The aftermath of my first tattoo wasn't nearly as hype as I thought it would be. He was sending a text and not paying attention to me much.

"No more breaking up, okay?" I said. In my voice there was hope and a need for reassurance.

"Okay, cool," he said. He reached over and gave me a pound with his fist.

As we drove, I looked down at my leg that was now tatted and taped down with a paper towel and saran wrap.

I returned to school and people were all over me with their opinions of my new tattoo. Some told me I was straight up stupid. Others asked things like "Did he get your name too?" and "What happens if you guys break up?" Even teachers asked me about it. I had my response ready — one that I thought was clever because no one was able to respond to it. "If I never leave him and he never leaves me then how are we breaking up?" I asked them.

One girl approached me, boldly, asking to see it. "I heard you got Carma's name on you," she said. She and I were cool so I turned my leg toward her so that she could see it. "That's tough! You're all that!" she said. She seemed to like it and I was happy to show it off either way.

Carma's mom asked to see it and I cringed at her response. "I don't know what is wrong with you young girls today, getting men's names tattooed on you. Carma does not belong to you. Carma is my child," she said.

It was only then that I felt stupid, so I didn't say anything. Besides, what could I say? She was Carma's mother and I was not about to disrespect her.

I made plans to visit my godsister, Cammy, that summer. "Bring me back some spices," was all my mom said to me before my departure. Toronto has a very, very large Caribbean population and my mom wanted me to bring her back some oxtail and curry seasonings.

I told her that I would try. "If I can find a store where they sell them, Mom," I said.

Her request was annoying because she kept repeating it constantly. "Ask your godmother!" Mom said, referring to Cammy's mom and one of her really good friends.

My mom and I were constantly butting heads. I resented her for everything I went through in the foster care system. I was mad at her for forcing me to pay rent. On top of that, I still had mixed feelings about the way she'd forced me to have an abortion when Quin ended up having a baby shortly after and had received my mom's full support. Though my sister's circumstances were entirely different from mine, there was still a hint of something negative that I was feeling toward my mom. Besides, I was going on vacation! I hadn't seen my godsister in years! It was Caribana weekend and Cammy promised me a week of fun, shopping and partying at all-ages events. *Who had time to visit Caribbean markets to search for these random spices?* I thought.

In attempts to ease Carma's mind about me leaving for a week, I asked him if he wanted me to bring him anything back from Toronto. He was very nonchalant about it but went on to tell me that he wanted sneakers and earrings — a pair of white Air Force 1 shoes and a small pair of gold hoops. I knew the sneakers would be easy to find because nearly every Foot Locker carried them. I also knew that finding the earrings would cause me a lot of anxiety, but I was determined to find the perfect pair. I wanted the earrings to be perfect and I wanted Carma to love them.

Before leaving, I went to Halifax Shopping Centre and stole a bunch of new clothes and shoes. I didn't want to spend my money because I knew I'd need it for the time that I was in Toronto. I was already giving so much money to my mom, I wanted to be sure that I had a lot of spending money for new clothes from stores that we don't have in Halifax, and for partying, of course. When the plane landed in Toronto, I was bursting with excitement. Cammy was waiting for me as soon as I got my bags. We jumped up and down and screamed out, "Heyyyy, sister!" It had been a long time since I'd seen her but I never separated her from my blood family, even though we weren't technically related.

I don't have a lot of childhood memories from when I lived in Toronto but I told Cammy about the earliest memory I could think of. We talked about picking petals off of dozens of flowers in her mom's front yard, playing the classic game called "He Loves Me, He Loves Me Not." We talked about how her mom had come outside yelling at us to clean up every single petal. Reminiscing about our younger years really had me feeling disconnected from that part of myself. Cammy told me a dozen stories, both funny and sad, that I had no recollection of, despite the small two-year difference in our age. She got me wondering about what my life would've been like if I had been raised in Toronto instead of Halifax. *What would my life be like without Carma? Who would I be?* As much as I tried, I couldn't imagine who that person would be.

By the end of the week, I was all partied and shopped out and ready to go home. I never did look for my mom's spices, but I found the sneakers for Carma, and after a lengthy conversation with a jeweler, I picked out what I thought were the perfect earrings. They were half gold and half rose gold, his favourite; not too big and not too small — just as he requested. I couldn't wait to go home and give them to him.

It was a few days before I saw Carma once I got back to Dartmouth, where I still lived with my mom, Quin and Meghan. I unpacked my things and left Carma's gifts on the floor, in their bags. My mom must've been snooping in my room and saw the bags of stuff because she began yelling at me over it.

"YOU COULDN'T EVEN BRING ANYTHING BACK FOR YOUR FAMILY BUT YOU BROUGHT THAT BOY BACK SOMETHING, DIDN'T YOU?" she screamed.

For whatever reason, I was feeling bold that day so I engaged in the argument. Normally I wouldn't have bothered, but she really pissed me off.

"I didn't know where to find your stupid spices. You shouldn't have been sneaking around in my room and you wouldn't know anything about what I got for *that boy*. You don't do nothing for me. I pay to live here. I put groceries in this house. Carma does more for me than you do!" I said.

Once she started calling me stupid and ungrateful, I blocked her out and went to my room to call Carma. He agreed to pick me up and I told him I would bring his gifts. Before leaving, I heard my mom call my dad, repeating what she had just said to me. She sounded loud, angry and ridiculous. My dad asked to speak to me and I broke out in tears due to my anger. He was trying to take her side, asking if it would have killed me to bring her home what she asked for.

"Carma's my own man," I said. Then, I told him exactly what I told my mom — "Carma does more for me than she does."

The argument with my mom continued and got even uglier. I couldn't stand her calling me names and telling me I was ungrateful. With my dad still on the phone, I yelled back at her: "WHAT DO YOU DO FOR ME? YOU NEVER RAISED ME! NOW YOU WANT TO BE MY MOM ALL OF A SUDDEN? ALL YOU CARE ABOUT IS MONEY AND YOURSELF!" I hollered.

When Carma got there, I left. We went for a drive in his dad's minivan and I told him what had just happened. He didn't take her side but he didn't take my side either, which caused an argument between the two of us.

"That is your mom though," he said.

"I really don't care," I told him. I was angry that he didn't automatically agree with what I was saying. And he wasn't tolerating my attitude.

It was nighttime and he had driven down a dark side street that was on a hill. At the bottom of the hill was a silver fence glowing in the moonlight. There was some construction going on down there. Beyond the fence was the Halifax Harbour. I was afraid of the dark and he knew that. "Do you want to get out of my car?" he asked.

I gave him a death stare. "Put me out," I said.

Click! He unlocked the door. "Get out," he said, looking straight at me.

I opened the door, planning to slam it shut. Before I could do so, he threw the black and white striped Foot Locker bag that contained his sneakers and earrings at me.

"*I* don't want them," I said.

"Neither do I," he replied.

I picked up the bag and began walking up the hill. The harbour was making the summer night's breeze colder than it ought to be. I folded my arms across my chest to block out some of the cold and contain my anger as best I could.

Carma drove away. When I got closer to the top of the hill some minutes later, I saw that he had stopped the van. I got closer to him and he rolled down the window to taunt me.

"Excuse me, miss, are you lost?" he asked.

I had to hold back my smile because I was so angry I almost started laughing.

He continued taunting me, driving beside me as I walked. "Aww, baby, are you cold? Do you want to come back in the car? Come back in the car," he said.

I told him no and kept walking. This went on for a minute or two until he got mad and pulled over completely to get out of the car and confront me.

"Get back in the car," he ordered.

"No, you put me out on the cold, dark street so now I'll walk home. Bye!" I said.

After trying to make a joke about me being his sulky baby, he got annoyed with me and took the bag out of my hand so that he could grip me in a bear hug. I started crying.

"Are you mad at me, baby? Come, let's get back in the car," he said.

I said, "Don't do that to me ever again," and we climbed back into the van.

He kept the sneakers but ended up giving away the earrings that I had picked out for him. He claimed they were "girl earrings."

That would be the last time I saw him for a while. My mom was sleeping when I got back in the house and when I left for work early the next morning. Sometime during the afternoon portion of my shift, I got a call from Quin.

"Mom told me to tell you don't come back and you ain't getting none of your stuff," she said. In the background, my mom was cursing and yelling.

"Fuck, man," I said aloud.

My co-worker looked at me and mouthed the words, "What happened?"

I hung up the phone and told her that my mom had just kicked me out. I started to have a panic attack in the gift shop. "I have to go," I told her.

She offered to cover for me by telling our boss that I had a family emergency. It kind of was. I called my dad and he told me to come to his apartment.

"I'm about to make supper anyway. Do you like steak?" he asked.

I quickly changed out of my uniform and hopped on the bus to go to my dad's apartment. Once I got there and had calmed down, I had a conversation with him.

"Well, you can stay here, Jadey. I would never see you out on the street. There's not much room but I'm usually out anyway. You can sleep in my room with me or on the couch, it's up to you," he said.

He knew, from experience, how crazy my mom could be. I thanked him and we sat down for supper, listening to his old country tunes. After we finished, he said he was going to see his buddy down the road and asked if I would be okay there by myself. I assured him that I would be fine and he told me that he would call and check up on me. When he left, I called Carma. Our initial conversation was short. I told him the story and I could practically hear the thought wheels turning in his head.

"Let me make a few calls and call you right back. Don't worry, I'll figure something out," he said.

I felt really relieved. I imagined that he would ask his mom if I could stay with them. *I wouldn't mind that*, I thought.

When he called me back, I was not prepared for his solution to my problems. "I spoke to my uncle in Montreal. He said you can stay with him and his girl," he said.

"Montreal?" I asked, completely confused.

"Yeah, but you can't stay there for free. You'll have to work," he declared.

"Get a job or work-work?" I asked. I had to clarify because where we come from, *having a job* and *working* are two different things — *having a job* meant that you were employed and earned a paycheque, *working* meant that you were a stripper.

"Work-work," he confirmed.

"What about school?" I asked. I was due to start grade eleven in a few weeks.

"My uncle's girl can get you a job at the strip club she works at. School can come later. You're young. Right now, you need to worry about yourself and where you're going to live," he said.

"Who's your uncle?" I asked.

When he told me who his uncle was, I immediately became alarmed. I had been told by elders in my community that Carma's uncle was one of the notorious pimps mentioned in the book *Somebody's Daughter*. The book tells of the horrible, inhumane things he'd done to the prostitutes who worked under him. I told Carma that I was scared based off what I had heard.

"Ain't nothing for you to be afraid of," he said. "He's my family and you're with me so ain't nothing gonna happen to you."

I told him that I wasn't sure and he told me he would let me think about it and to get back to him. I needed to talk to my friends. I called Laila and told her that I needed to talk to her and Jordan.

"Come over. Jordan's on her way here anyways," she said.

I called my dad to tell him where I was going and went on my way shortly after he got home.

Once I got to Laila's house, we all sat on the bed and I told them the whole story about my mom and what Carma said.

"So he wants you to be a stripper?" Laila asked.

"Well, how do you feel about it?" Jordan asked next.

I weighed out the pros and cons that I could think of and listed them out loud. "Well, I love dancing and I'll get to wear cute bikinis. I get to move to a new city. Maybe it will be fun. Only thing is, I'll have to live with his uncle and his uncle's girl and Carma won't be there the whole time because he'll still be living down here," I said.

"What about your mom?"

"Fuck her. She should have thought about that before she kicked me out," I said.

Laila and Jordan told me that as long as I was happy, they supported my decision. "Just be safe," Jordan said.

"I will be, I am happy," I said.

We dropped the topic and just hung out, taking pictures.

When Carma texted me, I told him I still needed time to think. Later on that night, I returned to my dad's apartment. I ended up telling Carma that I couldn't accept his uncle's offer because I would be staying with my dad, and there was no way that my dad was going to let me do that.

"It's cool. I was just trying to help," he said.

For the rest of the summer, I stayed with my dad. It wasn't so bad minus his asking if I was on the phone with a boy every time he saw me with the phone to my ear. *He was such a dad!* I didn't tell him about what Carma had suggested for fear of his response.

Quin managed to sneak some of my clothes out of my mom's house to help me get by. Because the rest of my belongings were not given back to me, I had to steal some more clothes from the mall. Quin was the only one to visit me. Whenever she came over, we would dance in my dad's living room or hang out with the two girls who lived down the hall.

Despite the chaos that had been going on in my life, I returned to school. Each day, I took the bus to the hood to meet Quin so that we could walk to school together. My mom moved back to Halifax, throwing out the rest of my things in the process. She even threw out my binder full of poetry that I had written and kept safe since I wrote my first poem. When I found out that she had done that, I gave her the silent treatment. I would see her on the bus and walk past her like a stranger. Whenever I went by to pick up Quin, I would stay in the laneway, on the other side of the fence, never entering her property.

One day, she was having people over for drinks when I stood at my usual spot near the fence, waiting for Quin. My mom tried to smile at me and I looked away, ignoring her.

"Ain't that something? My own child won't even speak to me," she said to her friend.

I scrunched up my eyebrows to show that I was not interested in her pity party. *It's her own fault*, I thought.

My mom went inside and her friend walked over to where I was standing. "Talk to your mother. Do you know how much it's hurting her to have her own daughter treat her like a stranger?" she said.

"I. Don't. Care," I said as if speaking to someone who couldn't hear too well.

I scrunched my eyebrows again, rolled my eyes and shrugged by shoulders to prove my point. The lady walked away from me, shaking her head.

Sometime after that, I was down the hall from my dad's apartment, hanging out with my neighbour when all of a sudden police lights flashed red and blue through her living room window. We both looked at each other. I continued eating my nachos while she went to see what was going on.

"Jade, isn't that your dad?" she asked.

I ran to the window just in time to see my dad, in handcuffs, being pushed into the back of the police car. I had no idea what was going on.

"Do you want to go downstairs?" she asked.

"No. He always does this shit," I said, holding back tears. I went to his apartment and cried. My dad had just been released from prison not too long before, and just like every time before then, he had promised that he wouldn't go back. I cried because he was gone again and because now I had to figure out where I was going to live . . . *again*.

This time, before I called Carma, I called Daneen.

"Want me ask my mom if you can come stay with us?" she asked.

"Please!" I told her.

Daneen's *mom* was actually her grandmother who had raised her since she was a baby. She was a sweet old woman who loved to cook and loved to see us eat her cooking even more. Almost with no hesitation, her mom agreed to have me come to stay.

"Mommy loves you, ya know. I asked her if you could come because your mom kicked you out and she said 'Yeah, tell her get her butt down here,'" Daneen told me. "Did you know your mom called me and told me she would call the police if I let you stay here?"

All I could do was shake my head.

"She told me she'd call Laila and Jordan too and tell them the same thing," Daneen said.

I was so frustrated and I began to hate my mom even more.

It took no time getting comfortable at Daneen's house. I had already spent so much time there that I was just like family. Because I was still a ward of the court in the foster care system, I still had to call my social worker to get permission to live at Daneen's house. Daneen's mom also had to sign some paperwork in order to receive money for food and toward rent. She told me that she wasn't going to charge me to live there but I told her she might as well accept the money since they were willing to provide it. I had my own room too, so everything was good except that me and Carma were ready to break up yet again. I don't know what it was about this time and I didn't care. I was so tired of all the back and forth bullshit.

CHAPTER 7

A LITTLE VACATION

I was working at Tim Hortons when I first met another guy. He charmed me like you'd see in a cheesy movie while he ordered his food and then asked for my number. I told him no but he said he wasn't leaving until he got it and there were people in the lineup, so I quickly wrote my number on a napkin and said, "Okay! Now get out of my line!" as I laughed. Once the lineup was gone, I went over the encounter in my head. His name was Reco. It wasn't really the first time I'd met him, but it was the first time we'd talked. He was from my hood, but he was older than me, so our circles didn't mix. I questioned if I'd done the right thing by giving him my number but ended up dismissing the thought. Carma didn't want to be with me and I knew he was already talking to other girls, so I decided it was time for me to do the same thing.

Reco and I hit it off right away. He called me Homegirl and I called him Homeboy in return. From the day I'd given him my number, we spent every day together. After an altercation with his mom, who thought I was too young for him, she began to accept me too. But, not before verifying my age!

Reco was fun. He let me take ecstasy pills — something Carma hated. We would laugh and talk for hours. I stayed over at his house every other night, and even when I didn't he was only "a hop, skip and jump away" as he would say. We lived a five-minute walk from each other. Reco was a dope boy and pretty well known in my hood. I didn't mind. Drug dealers were nothing new to me. Carma sold drugs. My dad had gone to jail for selling drugs.

It was no surprise when Carma ended up texting me, but I would tell him that I was busy watching a movie or something. It was like he had a sixth sense for when I was with another man. Still, I held my ground. He needed to know that he couldn't just leave and come back whenever he felt like it.

One evening, Daneen invited me and Quin to a basketball game. It was to be a rival game between Carma's school and another high school where I knew plenty of people. It was what we called a black game (where both teams were predominantly black) so, of course, we just *had to* be there. I agreed to go. If Carma was there, I knew he wouldn't talk to me in public. I got dressed up in a really cute outfit and went to see Reco before I left. He looked at me real seductive-like, with his eyebrow raised and asked why I was so dressed up if it was only a basketball game. I told him I would be back and he kept staring at me like he wanted to say something else.

"What?" I asked.

"I really care about you. Make sure you come back. Don't cheat on me or I'm choking you," he said with a playful smirk on his face.

I gave him a kiss and went to catch the bus. The game was uneventful in that I didn't see Carma. Afterward, I went to Reco's house just like I said I would.

Time went on and Reco and I continued to get along. We'd started having sex pretty early on. Sometimes we used protection and sometimes we didn't. I was on birth control and I trusted him because I knew him for so long, so it wasn't really an issue for me. One time though, I noticed some weird discharge when we were having sex. It didn't burn or smell too bad so I just waited for it to go away.

Carma had begun texting my phone regularly, saying he wanted me back. I told him that I was talking to someone else and he became even more persistent. He wanted me to come see him.

No. You can come see me, I texted back.

When he told me that he didn't have a car, I told him to take the bus, just to be an asshole. I didn't think he would actually do it, which is why I'd said it, but to my surprise he showed up. That was the first time Carma had ever taken the bus to come see me. We went to the mall to talk and when we got on the subject of me attending driving school, he agreed to pay for it.

"Just come home," he said, meaning he didn't want to be broken up anymore. Home was him. Home was us together. I thought I heard so much sincerity in his voice that I decided to go back to him.

It was difficult for me to leave Reco when he hadn't done anything wrong so I continued talking to him while attending driving school and being back with Carma. I didn't want to hurt his feelings; it wasn't about his "threat" to choke me. During the second weekend of driving school, I got a call from one of my girl friends telling me that Reco's ex-girlfriend was saying they were back together and that she wanted to speak to me. I gave my girl permission to give the other girl my number and she called me, basically stating her case that she and Reco were still together. I told her that Reco had told me they weren't together. She put some cards on the table about him and her — information that was indisputable. After that, it was easier to go home to Carma. I simply told Reco I was back with my man. By this time, my discharge had gotten worse and began to smell foul.

Carma invited me to stay over. I didn't want to go because of my discharge problem, but I felt like it would be suspicious if I refused so I went anyway. It was only a matter of time before Carma initiated the sex. I could tell how bad he wanted it. We started kissing. Inside my head, I was screaming at myself, knowing I should tell him. Right before he lowered himself down to give me what he said "would have been the best head I'd ever gotten in my life," I stopped him. Tears started rolling down my cheeks.

"What's wrong?" he asked.

"I think I have something. My discharge is weird and it smells," I said.

He wiped my face and kissed me. "If you have something then I have it too. Whatever it is, we'll get it cleared up. Don't even worry about it," he said.

We had sex, but I couldn't help but wonder *how* he had taken it so lightly.

In the morning, he ran us a bath. Bad idea. As soon as we got out to dry off, it felt like my vagina was on fire. It burned so badly I could barely stand it. I held a cold cloth on it until it subsided to a tolerable level. The same day, I went to see the doctor. Within a week, I got a call confirming that I did have something — chlamydia. I also had a yeast infection.

I cried. I felt dirty and betrayed. "Carma is going to kill me," I told Serena, a girl I hung out with at school. She asked if I got it from Carma or Reco. I blinked back tears. I'd assumed that I got it from Reco but she explained how you could have it and not have any symptoms and that something or someone could trigger you to start getting symptoms. I stopped crying, remembering how quickly Carma had been willing to dismiss the idea of me having an STI. At the point that I told him I thought I had an STI, he was unaware of me having sex with Reco. When I asked Carma if he had been with anyone else, it started a whole new argument. It was impossible to know who the culprit was.

I got the antibiotics for Carma and I, and went to spend the night with him again. I was on the fence about telling Reco because I didn't know who had given me the infection. I put myself in his shoes and realized I would want to know if I were him so I sent him a text that said: *I know you're probably going to blame me but I got chlamydia so you should go to the doctor and get checked.* At first, he was bitter and cold toward me, telling me that I must've gotten it from "one of the other guys I was fucking." A few weeks passed before Reco texted me again, saying he'd been to the doctor. *Good looking out, Homegirl,* was all the message said. That was the last time we spoke.

Anyway, everything was cool when Carma and I discussed contracting the STI. He said he had used condoms when he and I were broken up. I casually said that I should have done the same, thinking we were having an open, honest, judgement-free conversation. He jumped up and stood over me in a threatening way as I sat on the couch.

"You never used a condom?" he asked. His eyes were bulging out of his head and there was anger in them.

I started laughing. "No. How do you think I got the STI, through the condom?" I asked.

I was still laughing, not knowing why he was so angry. Before I could think about it any longer, he started punching me in the ribs.

"You think it's funny?" he demanded, over and over.

I was so shocked at what was happening and how fast he snapped that I went right on laughing. I tried to block his punches and squirm out from beneath him. When it really began to hurt, I stopped laughing and got mad. "Ouch! Get off me!" I said loudly.

In the next instant, his hands were around my neck. His palms were rough. He'd called them "working man's hands." Sometimes he'd have callouses from working in his parents' yard or with his uncles and occasionally from going to the gym. The hands that now suffocated me were the same hands that I'd rubbed lotion into with all of the tenderness I knew how to give. Automatically, I struggled to breathe under his grip. When he spoke, his pupils expanded, causing the brown colour of his eyes to disappear. All I saw was black in them. I was terrified, grasping his wrists to try to loosen his hold on my throat. With each sentence, each question, he strangled me harder.

"You think this shit is funny? I fucking love you and you're out here fucking the next man raw? You're gonna sit up here and laugh in my fucking face when you gave me a disease? I have to take pills and you think it's a joke? Do you think this is a fucking game?" he snarled. His words were loud and vicious.

I dropped my hands from his wrists, ready to allow myself to pass out. Finally, he let me go and I slumped to the floor, coughing. I don't know how I maintained consciousness — my throat felt like it was broken. My voice was raspy. His eye colour returned back to normal and he went to get me some water.

"Here. Drink this," he said.

I took the cup, staring at him, scared to death. "Where did you go?" I asked him, referring to what had happened with his eyes. "Your pupils took up your whole eye. Your eyes went black," I told him.

"Really?" he asked. "That's fucked. I never felt it. You just made me so mad. Don't ever disrespect me like that again," he said.

I sat in silence for a few minutes. "You could have killed me just now. You literally were not here. The devil was right in you," I said.

"Stop that. I wouldn't kill you. I love you too much. Let's go to bed," he said.

Afraid to do anything else, I followed him to the bedroom. Under doctor's orders, we weren't allowed to have sex for a few weeks so we just laid there until we fell asleep. I wondered if he could feel the tension in my body.

Taking a spare blanket, I crept back into the living room to sleep on the couch once I knew that he was asleep. In a matter of minutes, he was standing over top of me, demanding to know what I *thought* I was doing.

"I don't want to sleep with you," I said.

"You better get back in the room. You're not sleeping out here," he said.

When I refused, he took the blanket and hauled me to my feet. I stood there, not moving.

"I'm tired. Get back in the room," he said.

Since I was still ignoring his orders, he shoved me toward the room. Reluctantly, I climbed back onto the bed. He made sure to put me on the side closest to the wall this time. I was shaken up but I went to sleep anyway.

* * *

Just before winter turned into spring, I had my seventeenth birthday. It was still very cold and there wasn't much to do at that time of year so instead of hanging out with my girl friends, Carma made my day extra special. He bought me a plaid jacket in his favourite colour, took me to get my nails done and we went out for supper. He got us a bottle of alcohol and we spent the night at his house, having drinks and making love. March break was just around the corner.

"My uncle is driving down here from Montreal and he said we can drive back up there with him," Carma said.

"Do I have to work?" I asked him, wondering if he expected me to go to the strip club there.

"No, you don't have to work. We're just gonna go up there and check it out, like a little vacation," he said.

I thought about how romantic it would be to wander the streets of Montreal with him. "Okay, but I have to let Daneen's grandmother know and I have to call my social worker and ask," I said.

Daneen's mom was hesitant but she agreed to let me go if my social worker permitted it. I was reluctant to talk to my social worker about it because I knew she would bog me down with a million rules. I called her anyway and was right in guessing that she would want to know every aspect of my trip, down to the minutest detail. I approached the situation as if I were speaking hypothetically. "What if I wanted to leave the city for March break, what do I have to do in terms of dealing with the legalities?" I asked.

"You have to let me know where you're going, who you're staying with, the number of where you're going," said my social worker, Geanne. As a ward of the court, the system was legally responsible for me, so it was highly unlikely that I could just leave the province with my sixteen-year-old boyfriend.

At the age of seventeen, with all the hatred in the world for the system's rules, I caught an attitude while trying to explain that I was going out of town with my boyfriend and that we would be staying with some of his family. When I realized that she was sounding hesitant to let me go, I got mad. She talked about how it was a safety precaution to know where I was going to be.

"How can you tell me I can't go with my boyfriend? Why do I need to give you all these details? It's not for my safety. Of course I'm going to be safe," I snapped at her.

"Those are just the rules," she said.

I slammed down the phone. As long as someone knew where I was, I didn't care what my social worker said. I told Daneen's mom that I was going anyway.

"Well, I can't stop you. Just call me when you get there. I'll talk to your social worker when she calls," she said.

Still feeling heated from the conversation with Geanne, I called Carma so that I could vent. He sounded just as mad as I was.

"You don't need them in your life. Why don't you just sign out of care? Can't you do that?" he asked.

"I could but they pay Mrs. Brown for me to stay there and they take care of lots of other stuff too," I said.

"I'll take care of you. You're almost eighteen years old. They can't keep telling you how to live your life. How ya supposed to live?" he asked.

As frustrating as it was to be told what to do, I didn't really want to sign out of care so I told him that I was going to go anyway and that Mrs. Brown had said it was okay. He came over to help me pack, and a few days later a bunch of us piled into his uncle's van en route to Montreal.

In the van, it was me, Carma and his four little cousins in the back and his two uncles in the front. The notorious uncle whom I'd been told was described in *Somebody's Daughter* was driving. When I met him, I was unable to tie him to the image they painted of him in the book. He wasn't scary at all. In fact, he was very polite and good looking for his age. He offered to put my bags in the van and made a joke about how much stuff females always pack for a short trip.

"Well, I don't know what I'll need!" I giggled.

I remember looking into his eyes and not being able to put my finger on what it was that I saw. His eyes were dark brown but there was something else there too, beneath the colour of them. The whole time, I kept it in my mind that at least at some point, this man had been very dangerous to women. In attempts to protect myself, I made it a point to show no fear around him. Whenever he looked at me, I looked straight back into his eyes and made sure to speak for myself.

The drive to Montreal was long and brutal. The kids were extremely annoying. I never really had the capacity for children. They took turns pummeling me with silly questions, stretching my patience to its limits. The youngest cousin had the right idea: all she did was throw temper tantrums and sleep. After how long Carma let their interrogation go on, I was about ready to do the same thing. Carma and his uncles were taking turns driving, so sometimes I was stuck back there with the kids and an uncle, by myself. I was thankful when we stopped for bathroom breaks where Carma bought snacks and I got to stretch my legs. At one stop, Carma bought a huge bag of chips and told me to hold them while he drove.

"Don't give any of the kids my chips," he said.

In a split second, I was annoyed at the predicament he'd put me in. As soon as we pulled off, four little hands shot out. "Can I have some?" they all asked.

Not wanting to seem like a bitch on an already painfully long drive, I told them they could have *a few* chips. I opened the bag and watched in amused horror as they all shoved both hands in the bag. *Oh my gosh, Carma is going to snap*, I thought. Before I could get the last hand out of the bag, it was nearly empty. To make matters worse, Carma's uncle yelled up to the front that the chips were gone and busted out laughing.

"Jade, you let them eat my chips?" Carma called out.

"I didn't mean to!" I said as innocently as possible.

He never said anything else so I thought I was off the hook. Wrong. Some hours later, when we stopped again and he got in the back, he put his arm around my shoulders. "You let them guys eat my chips?" he whispered. The kids were preoccupied with something or another.

"Well, what did you want me to do? I didn't want them to hate me over some chips," I said. I felt like I was being scolded.

"I ain't lying, she did say only take a few," one of the kids said.

I smiled at him as Carma teased them about buying him a new bag of chips. Looking back to me, he got serious. "How can I trust you out here if I can't even trust you to watch my chips?" he asked.

"Wow, of course you can trust me! It's not that serious," I said defensively.

"Next time I tell you to do something, you better do it. I don't care who tells you different, okay?" he said.

I rolled my eyes, feeling like a rebellious teenager being lectured by her parent. "Okay, fine," I said.

"Now give me a kiss," he replied.

As if on cue, the kids all shrieked in disgust.

Carma kissed me again and said, "So what? That's my own woman!" We all started laughing.

Bored would be a measly descriptor if I were to try to describe how I felt sitting in the back of that van on the long drive to Montreal. I was more than bored — I was going a little crazy in my brain. As the kids slept, I sat there restless.

"Carma," I whined.

I guess this was his way of easing my agitation but he started pushing his hands down my pants. I'd made sure that I wore joggers for the trip so I would be somewhat comfortable.

"Oh my god, don't!" I whispered.

"Shhh, relax," he said, continuing.

I put my head on his shoulder and closed my eyes, putting my hands down his pants as well. We sat like that for a while, stroking in silence.

Finally, we reached Montreal. I was exhausted. All I could think about was showering and sleeping. Carma's uncle showed us where we could sleep — it was an empty room besides a rickety dresser and an air mattress on the floor. The walls were barren. I don't even remember there being a window. I groaned on the inside.

Just then, the uncle's girl was introduced to us. I tried not to let my jaw drop when I saw who it was. "This is Shana," his uncle said. Standing in front of me was the girl I had beaten up when I was dating Jody.

I don't know how long Carma, his uncle and Shana waited for me to say hello. I let her make her move first. She said 'hi' and I said 'what's up,' very straight-sounding. I gave her eye contact, without smiling, to let her know that I hadn't forgotten about our fight. When Carma and I were alone, I told him how I knew her.

"Don't even worry about it. I'll tell my uncle to tell her not to say anything," he said.

When Carma returned from that conversation, he said his uncle would speak to her and there would be no problems.

"Let me know if she tries to say anything and I'll deal with it," he said.

I shrugged my shoulders. "Okay."

What alarmed me most about seeing Shana was two things: I had an unresolved beef with her, as she had called me out to fight a second time but it didn't end up happening. The other was that Shana and I had to have been the same age. Either that or she was younger than me. That would have been fine, except Carma's uncle was easily in his forties. I decided to ask Carma about it.

"Why is she here?" I asked.

"What do you mean? She lives here," he replied.

"Yeah, but why is she here with your uncle?"

"She works," Carma said.

I asked him if he meant she *work-worked*.

"Yeah," he said.

"Like, at a strip club?" I asked.

"Yeah," he replied.

"Oh, that's weird," I told him.

"What's weird about it?" he asked.

I pointed out that she was our age.

"Ya gotta eat. If ya don't eat, you'll die," he replied.

"I guess so," I said.

That night, I saw Shana leave to go to work.

The whole week that we were in Montreal, I barely saw Carma. Each day he was gone, I went a little crazier. He was always out with his uncle or one of his cousins. He even drove to Toronto and stayed there overnight. He would leave me with no food and little money.

Forced to be in the house alone together with Shana, I struck up a conversation with her. "Do you have to go to work every day?" I asked her.

"Yeah, but sometimes I don't go just so he'll get mad and come here to fight with me," she said.

"I'm hungry," I told her.

"Let's go to the store," she suggested.

I told her I didn't have any money and she said it didn't matter. "Don't you have to go to work?" I asked.

"I ain't going," she said.

We survived off Domino's Pizza, bought with the twenty bucks Carma would sometimes leave me. It was either that or instant noodles or rice that Shana and I managed to steal from the dollar store down the street.

After a while, Carma and his uncle came storming in. Carma pulled me into the room. "What were you guys doing?" he demanded.

"Nothing, we went to get some food," I said.

"You can't just leave like that. You have to tell me where you're going," he said.

Just then, his uncle came in the room. Looking at me, he said, "Please don't be following behind that girl. She knows what she's allowed to do and what she ain't."

"Okay," I said.

He left the room and I could hear him arguing with her. I felt bad for her; I was the one who had been hungry. She ended up having to go to work anyway. Carma left with them and I was left by myself, again — bad idea.

I was filled with rage. I sent him a text. *This ain't no kind of vacation. All you do is leave me here by myself so you can go run the roads with your uncle.*

I have to be out here. We will talk when I get back, he replied.

There was no way I was letting him off the hook that easy. In fact, it made me angrier. *What are you doing that's so important that you have to leave me for hours/days by myself with no money and nothing to do?* I cried as I texted this. I felt so dismissed and unimportant.

I gotta be out here so I can get money for us to eat.

I texted that he might as well send me home if this was all he was going to do because I didn't come to Montreal so that I could sit in the house by myself. *I could've did this at home; I want to do something fun.*

He promised we would do something when he got back. I waited and waited. I didn't know what to do with myself. Sadly, I started making excuses for his absence. I sent him another text. *Are you just doing this so when I work, I'll know how to be by myself, in case you can't be there with me?*

Yes. See, you already know so why you getting mad? You're so smart; I don't even have to tell you, he replied. His answer satisfied me.

It was getting late so I told him I was going to sleep and that I'd see him when he got back. *I love you*, I sent.

Love you too, baby, he texted back.

I tossed and turned all night. When I got up in the morning, the bed was still empty beside me. He came in some time later. "Get up, let's go out," he said.

"Where are we going?" I asked.

"For a bike ride," he replied.

I'd thought he was kidding but he pulled two bikes out of the shed. Off we went, cycling and laughing. We biked around until we got hungry. There weren't very many options in the area so we opted for stuffed-crust pizza from Pizza Hut. Carma carried it back to the house, one hand on the handlebars.

After we ate and had sex for what seemed like the first time since we'd gotten to Montreal, he was ready to leave again. I started crying, saying I wanted to go home. In an instant, he had me pinned down on the air mattress with his hands around my throat. "Why do I always have to fucking argue with you?" he spat through gritted teeth. "Just once, can you shut the fuck up and let me do what I'm doing?"

All I could muster was, "Get off of me."

He let go. "I hate when you get me like that," he said.

"You get yourself like that. You're crazy!" I told him.

He left. I went to take a shower.

When he returned the next day, I had my bags packed, fully prepared to leave. He was with his cousin and had only come to change his clothes. "Hold on," he said to his cousin, who didn't acknowledge me before he disappeared somewhere to wait for Carma.

Carma went into the bathroom. "Get in here and sit down," he demanded, pointing to the toilet seat cover.

I sat. As always, his hands went straight to my throat. I busted out crying.

He lifted me to my feet by my neck. "Why do you always do this shit? What's wrong with you?" he asked me.

"I don't want to be alone. You always leave me. Let me go," I sobbed.

He apologized and removed his hands from my throat where his nails had been digging into my skin, again. "I'm sorry. We're gonna go home soon, okay? Come get in the shower with me," he said.

I slowly took off my clothes.

"Stop crying," he said.

We got in the water. If we had ever had make-up sex before, it was nothing compared to that day. He kissed me softly on my lips. The water was so hot; I could barely breathe from all of the steam. His strokes were deep. He put his palm on my throat and held me like that, like I was the only thing keeping him from evaporating into the steam. The water stung the nail marks on my neck.

"I'm sorry, okay?" he pleaded through whispers.

"Me too, I'm sorry too," I replied in the same tone.

We exchanged 'I love yous.' With my back against his chest, I sobbed quietly into the shower wall. We finished and I was too tired to argue about him leaving again.

His cousin said, "All right, Jade, see ya later," and they were gone again.

CHAPTER 8

OWNERSHIP

I can't remember how we got home, but we made it back from Montreal. Things went back to normal, whatever our normal was. We both went back to school after the break. It was a few days before either of us talked to each other. I guess we needed to recuperate from our trip.

I became depressed again. I quit my job and seriously spoke to the staff at MAP about quitting school as well. I was just too tired of it all. My social worker blamed it on the birth control injections I was taking.

I would sleep over at Carma's house and barely have the energy to talk to him. "What's wrong?" he'd ask.

Very dryly, I would say, "I don't know. I just feel sad."

He asked me if I wanted a codeine pill. The pills were left over from having surgery on his shoulder after a car accident, years before I met him.

"How come you still have them?" I asked.

"I took them but they made me feel too drowsy so I stopped. I just threw them in my drawer and let my shoulder heal on its own," he said.

"Didn't it hurt without the pills?" I asked.

He shrugged and said yeah, as if it wasn't a big deal. "I'm only giving you one though. They're very addictive. I hate seeing you like this. You look right lifeless," he said.

I agreed to take one. Soon, my fingertips were tingling and my nose started to itch. "My nose is itchy," I said, scrunching up my face.

"It did that to me too, that's why I stopped taking them. I felt like a crackhead," he said.

I lay down and went to sleep. When I woke up, the induced cloud of comfort was gone. Carma drove me home. In the car, tears rolled down my face for no apparent reason.

"Are you okay?" he asked.

"Just drive," I said.

Sometime later, Carma and I were driving down Woodland Avenue on our way home from a dinner date at Montana's Steakhouse in Dartmouth Crossing. We were arguing. I don't even know what we had been arguing about. Knowing us, it was probably about a girl.

"Okay, well, I'm not arguing with you anymore so you'll be arguing by yourself!" I said firmly to Carma. I pulled out my phone to check a text I had just received from one of my girls, intent on ignoring him.

"I'M TALKING TO YOU!" Carma yelled, snatching it away.

That was the last thing I remembered about the heated argument that had just taken place. Blackness. Pressure exploded around my left eye. My hands flung towards the pain. It felt wet.

"Fuck!" he said as I let out a groan.

He pulled over on Slayter Street. "Let me see," he said.

I heard my Keybo phone hit the floor of the car — the phone that he had just hit me in the face with.

"Get off me! Let me out!" I cried.

He unlocked the door and my torso fell out of the car, with me still half-sitting in my seat. My seatbelt held me mostly in place. The supper we'd just eaten came burning out of my throat and onto the curb. Finally, I was able to open my eye. The wetness I felt was my blood. It was dripping from somewhere near my eye and down my face. I squinted. It was all over my hands and the front of my jacket. I struggled to see.

"What did you do? What did you do?" I asked over and over, crying. I was in shock.

"Get back in the car," he demanded.

I hauled myself back into a seated position, holding my eye again and crying out in pain. I reached for my phone to call Daneen. When she picked up, I told her that Carma had hit me. "My eye is fucked, Daneen," I sobbed into the phone.

"Put him on the phone right now!" she ordered. I heard her yell at him, "WHAT DID YOU DO TO MY BEST FRIEND?"

As they talked, Carma drove off and pulled into the McDonald's parking lot. "Daneen, where are you? I need you to come get her right now. I can't let her go home like this. I'll put you guys up in a hotel," he said.

I took the phone. He went inside to grab some napkins for the blood. Once he was back in the car, he called one of his boys. "I need your key right now. I need to use your house," he said. His tone was frantic.

His friend told him where to find the key and he took me there. It was a five-minute drive from where we were. All I could do was cry. My tears mixed with my blood. I didn't know what to say. I didn't know what to do. My lips trembled. I don't know if it was me or the evening air that was cold, but I shivered.

When we got inside the apartment, I told him to move out of my way. I locked myself in the bathroom to examine my face in the mirror. I did not recognize who I saw. Some of my blood had already crusted over. My eye was swollen almost completely shut. My eyelid had quickly turned black. There was a gash beneath my eye where the phone had pierced my skin.

Just then, I heard Carma on the other side of the door. He was on the phone again. I heard him sniffling. *Crying?* I wondered. Panic was embedded in his voice. "Devin! Devin! I fucked up. I hit Jade, ya man. Her eye is split open," he said.

"Aw, ya man, why would you do that?" I heard Devin respond.

I sat down on the toilet seat cover.

BANG! BANG!

"Jade! Open the door. Let me see!" Carma hollered.

I didn't move until he threatened to kick the door open. I knew that he would so I got up to open it, not wanting to ruin his friend's apartment. I tried to move past him to get away. He grabbed my shoulders. "Let me see," he said again.

As I was struggling to get out of his grip, he bear-hugged me. "I'm so sorry," he kept saying. "Will you forgive me, please? Please, forgive me," he said.

I lifted my head to look at him. It looked like he had been crying.

I started crying again and struggling to get free from his grip but he wouldn't budge. "I hate you! Why would you do this to me? I hate you!" I sobbed.

I stopped fighting and let him hug me. It was either that or let my body collapse to the floor because I had no fight left in me at that point.

"Let me wipe your eye for you," he said, going into the kitchen to get a paper towel.

Before he could come near my eye again, I took the paper towel out of his hand and walked back into the bathroom.

"Don't lock the door!" he ordered.

"I'm not! Look at all this blood!" I exclaimed.

Wetting the paper towel, I began to slowly wipe the blood from my face, wincing in pain, and then worked on getting it off of my jacket.

Carma stood in the doorway, biting his nails. "I can't let you go home like this. I told Daneen I'll put you guys up in a hotel," he said.

"Just take me home. Please, take me home," I replied with an exhausted tone.

To my surprise, he agreed. We drove to my place. Before I got out of the car, Carma said, "I'll understand if you leave me but I hope you don't. I'll wait to see if you call."

I was glad that everyone was in bed when I got back to Daneen's grandmother's house. Daneen must've been at her boyfriend's place or something. I went straight to my room. The tiny bedroom looked massive that night. I didn't know what to do with myself so I climbed over the footboard and sat in the small space between that and the wall. I pulled out my phone. *I need to talk to someone*, I thought.

Daneen texted me. *Are you all right? Do you want me to come home?*

I didn't want *her* to see my eye so I said no. I was embarrassed and ashamed.

I sent a text message to Jordan in hopes that she could drive her mom's car to come and get me. *Jordan, Carma hit me. My eye is split open*, it read.

Oh my god! Are you serious? Where are you?

I'm home. He just dropped me off. Can you come get me?

I told you to leave him, you girl. I can't come there.

I dropped my phone on the floor. It took everything in me to refrain from crying again. I wanted to scream. I was mad. I was mad at Jordan and mad at myself. I was mad at Carma. I sat there, alone on my bedroom floor, contemplating what I should do. For no reason in particular, I called Zee, my former crush and Videll's older brother. I didn't know what I expected him to do but I didn't think twice when his face popped into my brain. When he picked up the phone, I nearly started crying at the sound of his voice.

"Hi, Smeltzy," he said. That was his nickname for me.

I asked him if he was busy.

"I'm just with my brother. Why, what's up? Why do you sound like that?"

I was holding back tears. "Carma hit me," I said.

"I'll be right there. Pack a bag and come meet me by the bus stop," he replied. His voice was extremely calm. He didn't ask me any other questions.

I threw on some jogging pants, put some clothes in a bag and went to meet him. When I got in the car, I could only manage a whispered hello.

"Are ya all right?" his brother asked.

I felt relieved. "I am now," I said.

We drove the rest of the way to their house in silence. It didn't occur to me that I would see Videll.

The care with which Zee treated me that night was incredible. He was gentle and comforting. He took our clothes off and pulled me into the shower. Although we had fooled around all the time so long ago, his usual sexual efforts were gone. This time, it was different. I let him wash my body in silence. We got out and he dried me off, telling me to sit on the bed. He left and returned with a cotton ball and rubbing alcohol to clean the gash under my eye.

"This might sting," he informed me.

I just sat there. Once it was clean, he kissed me right on my wound. My heart melted. I was so incredibly grateful. I was speechless. He laid me down and told me it was time to go to sleep. Then, he climbed into bed beside me. With both of us still naked, I fell asleep in his arms.

I'd always wondered if he cared for me or if the feeling was strictly physical. That night, I didn't question it. If he never loved me, it didn't matter. He loved me enough to save my life that night. I don't know what I would have done if I'd had to spend that night alone.

The next morning, I was afraid to go upstairs in their mother's house. Their mom was like a mother to me and Quin. She didn't play any games and I could only imagine what an earful I'd get when she discovered the source behind my war wounds — a war that I felt lost to. When I couldn't avoid it any longer, I walked upstairs and sat on the couch.

"Hi, Videll. Hi, Miss Jasmine," I said. I positioned myself so the two of them were on my right side.

"Oh, hey, boo! I didn't know you were here," Videll said.

Miss Jasmine didn't miss a beat. "Umm hi, Jade. Look at me for a sec."

I started grinning and turned to look at her.

"What happened to your face?" she asked.

Before I could answer, Zee answered for me. "Carma punched her in the face," he said.

Miss Jasmine's arms folded across her chest so fast, I could only laugh. Her lips gnarled up in the way that only her mouth can. "He. Did. *What*?" she asked through clenched teeth.

"He didn't punch me, he hit me with my phone," I said. I demonstrated it on Videll.

"What did your mother say?" Miss Jasmine asked.

I told her I hadn't seen her yet and that I didn't plan on telling her.

"And who's Carma?" Miss Jasmine asked.

"Umm, my boyfriend?" I said hesitantly. It sounded more like a question.

"Umm, you mean your ex-boyfriend?" Miss Jasmine replied sternly.

Videll sighed. "Oh, Jadekins," she said, using my mother's nickname for me.

For the next few minutes, we had to listen to what Miss Jasmine thought I should've done in the moment. I let her finish. I looked at her when she toned her voice down. Her lip had begun to relax out of its gnarled position. I could breathe again.

"Jade, honey, I know you probably don't want to right now but you have to leave him. It's only gonna get worse," she said.

All I could do was look away. I didn't have a response.

Soon after I spoke to Miss Jasmine, Zee drove me to the bus stop so that I could go home. While on the bus, I was contemplating how long I would have to avoid my mom before my eye was healed.

"HI, MY GIRL!" my mom yelled from across the street as if on cue.

I pulled my hood further over my face, waving back.

"Come see your mother!" she said.

Nervous as hell, I crossed the street. "Hi, Mom," I said.

"Why do you have your hood up like that, what's wrong?" she asked with an awkward laugh.

I pulled my hood off and my mom gasped when she saw the condition of my face.

"Oh my god, who hit you?" she said, astonished.

"Carma," I whispered, looking at my feet.

"Look at me when I'm talking to you! I know you didn't just say that little punk put his hands on my little girl," she said. "Wait right there." She cursed Carma and his mom's name to her girl friend whom she had been visiting with. "Watch when your father calls! I'm telling your brothers too!" she said.

"Can I go now, Mom? I want to go home," I said to her.

She gave me a hug and a kiss and permitted me to leave, telling me she'd be calling to check in with me later. I went home and had to explain everything all over again to Daneen's grandmother and aunt. Finally, I made it to my room. I chucked my bag on the floor and climbed under my covers, telling myself I was never waking up. But I knew that wasn't really an option. I had to get up to return to school. I had all sorts of feelings going on.

The shame and embarrassment never went away — neither did the anger. And now I was mad at the world too because all I wanted to do was lie down and die but I had to go on living anyway. It was like the day everybody saw my tattoo, only it was on my face and it was swollen, black, purple and the blood was still crusted over. I never smiled all day. When I saw Jordan in the hallway, I walked straight past her. I caught a glimpse of her big, green eyes and saw the shock peeking out from behind them.

The gash under my eye took about two weeks to heal. As the marks faded, I began to miss Carma. I felt like I had no one. I spoke to my dad, who had called from jail, and I think one of my brothers texted me. My brother Riley made threats against Carma but nothing happened. Nobody really protected me. I was on my own again, just like when my mom had kicked me out.

With a sore eye socket and no one to confide in, I went back to Carma. It was a while longer before I went back to his house though. I wasn't ready to face *his* mom. But I had to face her eventually.

"So you're back, are ya? You didn't have enough yet?" she asked.

I sat at the kitchen table, smiling, feeling stupid and probably looking even dumber to be there. I didn't have anything to say to her.

She kept on talking. "You should've called the cops on him," she said.

I shook my head.

"What, you scared? That's my son and I'm giving you permission. If he ever tries that shit again, lock his ass up. I didn't raise a woman beater. A man has no call putting his hands on a woman. I'm serious — if it happens again, call the police," she said.

"Okay," was my only response. She took a sip from her tea before she continued.

"Uh, uh! I wish Carma's dad would try some shit like that," she said, I think more to herself than to me.

Despite all that had happened, Carma and I continued to

be together. He promised me he would never put his hands on me again. Over the next while, I noticed two things. One, his promise to never hit me again had nothing to do with the actual pain that he had inflicted upon me — he promised this because he said I wasn't worth going to jail for. Two, he lied. He did hit me again, lots of times. Though he never did anything as drastic as punch me in the face (or hit me with a phone), he chose to choke me instead. Every time he got heated to a certain point during an argument, his hands would close around my throat. The other thing he would do was punch me in my ribcage until I begged and screamed at him to stop.

Our relationship continued on its roller coaster track. Sometimes, it was really, really good. We would spend days together, talking, laughing and seeming to enjoy each other's company. We even jogged together in his neighbourhood a couple of times. One sunny day, we ventured into the woods behind his aunt's house and found a small, natural waterfall. We cupped our hands together and drank water from it. We would have mind-blowing sex, then we'd go on dates to restaurants or the movies and stuff like that. Other days, it was unbearable. I'd be driven insane and be fully convinced that I was having a mental breakdown. I just never knew what to expect.

As I said before, Carma didn't allow me to drink or take drugs. The only time I was allowed to do so was when I was with him. We were both underage the night we attended a party in his hood. Daneen was there too. She and I got there first and Carma came later with his friends. When he arrived, he took Daneen and me to the bar to get a drink. I was sporting a purple dress that was halter-top style and I wore my hair in long single braids. My shoes matched my dress. Carma seemed more than happy to see me rocking his favourite colour. We all stood together, drinks in hand.

Daneen and I took a break from shouting out the lyrics to Too Short's song, "Blow the Whistle." Still vibing to the music, a group of older guys approached us to greet Carma. Some of them already knew Daneen. I had seen a few of them around. One of the guys, a well-known pimp, was eyeing me up and down as he gave Carma props and they began talking — about me. I sipped my drink and pretended like I didn't hear them shouting to each other over the music.

"Carma, that's you right there?" the guy asked, pointing to me.

"Yeah, man," Carma replied with his usual charismatic smile.

"Christ! You got something on your hands! Turn her around, let me see, man," the guy said.

Carma grabbed my hand and pulled me toward the group of guys standing around him. He spun me in a circle in front of them as they hooted and hollered their approval. My cheeks burned with embarrassment. He pulled me close to him and kissed me on the mouth while grabbing my butt, nearly exposing it. I pulled back, half laughing, trying not to embarrass him and knowing I wanted to retreat. When he let go, I walked back over to Daneen. I was so mad, but I knew I had to keep my composure. It wasn't until he said it was time to go that I was able to voice my disapproval — when we were out of earshot of the other guys.

"Why did you do that?" I asked.

"Do what?" Carma asked casually.

"Spin me in front of that guy. Why did you do that like I was for sale or something?" I replied.

He pulled me into an awkward, liquor-induced hug. "You ain't for sale. You're my baby, okay? I'm just proud to have you beside me. Look how good you look!" he said.

"Fine," I replied. I still felt uneasy somewhere in my belly but it was cold and raining and the walkway had turned to mud so I tiptoed my way to the car and we drove back to his house.

Another party I went to in Carma's hood landed me in trouble. This time, I wasn't with Carma but it was his friend's party so he let me go with my girls. While there, a guy called me a bitch and threatened to knock me out. I was drunk and showing him no fear. I told him if he touched me he better make sure he knocked me out cause I would call my boyfriend and get my younger brother to knock him out too. The argument went on like that for nearly thirty minutes until one of Carma's homeboys came stumbling over to where we were standing in the driveway outside of the party.

"Jade! What's going on?" he asked.

"This little boy said he's gonna knock me out so I told him to do it," I replied.

Carma's homeboy looked at the other guy and asked him if he knew who I was. There was amusement in his intoxicated voice.

"I don't give a fuck," the other guy replied.

"This is Carma's *girl*, right here. I can't let you do that," he told the guy who had threatened me.

"Carma who?" the guy asked.

"Carma!" he replied.

"Oh, shit! Say word, that's Carma's girl?" the guy said. His entire demeanor immediately shifted.

"Yeah, man! She's *been* with Carma. This is a real-ass bitch, right here. A real bad bitch! As bad as they come! Stays down for her nigga!" Carma's homeboy went on and on.

The whole time, I was just standing there while this conversation played out. I was still ready to fight with this guy.

The guy who threatened me suddenly extended his hand to give me props. "My bad, cuz. I didn't know you were Carma's girl. That's my family," he said.

Carma's homeboy told me to shake the guy's hand and excused his drunken, belligerent behaviour. Reluctantly, I reached out and grabbed his hand.

"I ain't lying, Carma got something. You're some bold," the perpetrator said.

"And I meant every word I said. I'm not scared of you," I told him.

"Nah, man. It's all good," he replied.

Both of us walked away. I guessed Carma's name held some weight.

After the party, I went to Carma's house and told him everything that happened. I asked him if he would've come and defended me if I'd have called him.

"Yeah," he said, sounding annoyed that I would even ask that.

"What would you have done?" I asked eager to hear his response.

"I would have tried to talk it out with him and if he wasn't hearing me then it would have been a problem," he said.

I wasn't convinced. "Would you fight for me?" I asked.

"Yeah," he said.

By then, I tried to lighten the mood. "Can you even fight?" I asked, laughing.

He matched my playfulness and replied with, "Try me and see!"

We laughed and went to bed.

The school year dragged on. I was still feeling like quitting and depression lurked at the back of my mind. It felt thick in my throat and I often had trouble sleeping when I was alone. I always felt tired. It seemed like Carma and I could never get it right — at least, not consistently.

We had broken up, again. This time, I called Jody and asked him if we could spend the night together. Even though Carma was jealous of him and had forbade me to go near him, I went anyway. I just needed to distract myself. We hadn't been more than friends since I got involved with Carma anyway. He'd respected my boundaries when I told him I wasn't allowed to talk to him.

This time was different. Carma had left me for another reason unknown to me. All we did was argue with each other. I was truly convinced that he'd meant it this time and it was the *only* reason I called Jody. I had no idea that Carma would call me, but of course he did, right when I was sitting in the passenger seat of Jody's car. As soon as I saw Carma's name pop up on my phone screen, I knew I was going to be in really deep trouble. I looked at my phone, afraid to answer. It rang quite a few times before I picked up.

"Hello," I said.

"Yeah, what are you doing?" Carma asked.

"I'm driving," I told him.

"With who?" he asked.

"Why?" I asked with sheer attitude.

"I asked you a question. Now answer it," he said.

"I'm with Jody," I replied.

Right then, my phone hit the service dropout section of Up Home Road, which I had driven on with Carma over a hundred times. The call was lost.

Fuck! I thought. I looked at Jody with panic in my eyes. "He's gonna kill me," I said.

"Why? You guys ain't together," Jody said.

"I know we're not but he's about to go off, watch," I said.

I felt the tension building up deep in my belly. Carma tried to call me back but my phone kept cutting out. Then, the angry texts started rolling in. *So, this is what you're doing? We break up for what, a day? And you're gone to hop on the next man's dick!*

I texted him back and tried to sound more confident than I felt. *Why do you care? Didn't you leave me? I didn't want to be alone so I called Jody and I'm not fucking him so think what you want.* When we got out of the no cellphone service area, Carma called again. He sounded frantic. I could hear the angry pressure building up in him. "Where you at?" he asked.

"Pulling up to Jody's house," I said.

"You better get your ass over here, right now, if you want any chance of being with me again," he said and hung up.

I took a deep breath. Looking at Jody, I apologized and told him that I had to go. "He said I better come there right now," I said.

"All right," Jody sighed.

I handed him the bag filled with Burger King food that he had just bought for us. It was still hot. Carma's back door faced Jody's front door. It was a three-minute walk. Carma stood in the doorway, looking straight at me. I looked straight back at him as I walked with my overnight bag in my hand. I tried not to look down as if to appear guilty. I grinned. I was so nervous. *I didn't do anything wrong,* I assured myself. Still, I knew that his pupils had expanded, turning his eyes black. I knew it before I even got to the doorway. "Fuck, man," I said to the wind.

When I got inside his house, he took my bag and threw it onto the floor.

"Oh, you were planning on spending the night with him so you could get some dick, eh?" he asked.

"No I wasn't gonna get some dick. You left me. What did you expect me to do?" I said.

He started yelling and grabbed me by the front of my shirt. "I EXPECTED YOU TO STAY HOME AND FUCKING WAIT FOR ME TO CALL YOU. NOT RUN AROUND AND BE A FUCKING DOG!" he spat.

I told him to let me go but he didn't, not yet. "I didn't think you were gonna call," I said.

He let me go. "So all of a sudden you thought I wasn't gonna call but we end up talking every other time, right? But you couldn't wait this time. You probably never waited all them other times either, ya dirty bitch. Look at ya!" he said.

His words ricocheted from my ears into my heart, piercing it. "If that's what you think of me then why did you tell me to come here? You should've just let me go," I said.

He grabbed my bag and pushed it into my chest. "Leave then," he threatened.

I began to leave.

I can't pinpoint whether he sounded hurt, mad or both with what he said next — "So you're just gonna fucking leave?"

I turned around to face him. "You just told me to," I said.

He went on to call me every dirty, bitch, whore, slut and freak name he could think of before he was slightly more calmed down. "How am I ever going to trust you again if that's what you go and do as soon as we break up?" he asked.

I told him again that I didn't do anything.

He got freakishly calm. "Well, since you wanna be a freak,

be my freak. Let me and Jaylin run a train on you," he said. I laughed at him, knowing he must have gone completely mad. He couldn't really want me to have sex with him and his friend at the same time. I mean, that's what a train was.

"I'm not fucking you and Jaylin. I didn't do anything," I said.

"Then have Jaylin. Prove to me that you didn't fuck Jody," he said.

I looked at him in disbelief. Tears started falling down my cheeks. "You say you love me and you would make me fuck one of your best friends for no reason?" I asked. I was horrified. I picked my bag up and began to leave again.

"If you walk out right now, we're done and I mean it. Don't fucking come back!" he snarled.

I cried harder. I assessed what that would mean. I couldn't do it, I couldn't be without him. He was everything to me. I put my bag down, mentally putting myself down as well, in defeat. "Fine, I'll do it," I said.

He seemed to come to life then, suddenly very excited. "Stop crying cause you wasn't crying when you were out there being a dirty dog," he said.

I stood there in silence. There was no use arguing.

He called Jaylin and told him to come over. "I got a freak for us," he said.

When Carma hung up, I asked him if he was going to watch.

"Do you want me to?" he asked.

I replied "no" but he must've heard me wrong because he watched anyway. The basement got colder. My tears didn't feel warm on my cheeks anymore. Jaylin came over in what seemed like a split second. Carma pulled him to the side and whispered something I couldn't hear. I looked everywhere but at them. Just then, Carma walked up to me and asked if I was ready. I nodded my head. It was almost completely dark but Carma must've heard or sensed my sobs.

"Stop crying. You put this on yourself," he whispered. "Go ahead," he said to Jaylin.

Carma went and sat on the basement stairs. He sat with his elbows on the tops of his bent knees like a basketball player would sit on the bench, waiting to be subbed into the game.

"Take your pants off," Jaylin said to me.

I did as I was told. It was so cold; I crossed my arms across my chest to keep from shivering too noticeably.

"Lie on the couch," he said.

I lay down on my back and Jaylin climbed on top of me after taking off his shorts. From where I lay, I could see the whites of Carma's eyes. He was staring at us.

"Get me hard," Jaylin said. I reached down and complied. I don't know if he expected me to give him head but I wasn't about to do that. He got semi-hard and put a condom on.

"Turn over," he said.

I was thankful to be in doggy-style position. That way, I didn't have to look at Carma looking at me being fucked by his best friend. Jaylin started touching me. His fingers felt cold and foreign. He was digging them in hard and fast while stroking himself. I winced with each prod. Finally, he stopped and slid inside me. He wasn't very big so it wasn't physical pain but I felt emotionally hurt. My naked, goose-bump riddled backside slapped against his thighs. I started crying again. I couldn't contain myself.

I heard Jaylin start to say something. "What the —" he said. He slowed to a stop and laughed with what sounded like nervousness. "Aww no, Carma. I'm done. I'm done!" he said.

I grabbed my pants as soon as I was able to and slid them back on. Carma gave Jaylin props. I stood there wondering what had just happened. *Why did Jaylin stop like that? He couldn't see my face. Did he know I was crying?* I thought.

Jaylin turned to leave, closing the back door behind him.

Carma rushed over to me and grabbed me in a big hug. "Come here! You're a real fucking bitch!" he kept repeating, like it was a compliment. "You're the boss girl, I ain't never leaving you. Come here, give me a hug. Stop crying!" he said.

He tried to wipe my tears but I just cried harder. "I told you I didn't do anything!" I said again, desperate for his approval.

"I know, I believe you," he said. He was so happy.

I felt exhausted. "Why did you watch us?" I asked.

"I thought you wanted me to," he said.

I took a deep breath. "Can I go shower?" I asked. I was dying to be under the showerhead and feel the hot water on my skin.

"Yeah, stop crying. I love you, okay?" he said.

"I love you too," I said.

CHAPTER 9

THE GAME

I was hanging onto my sanity by a thread by the time school was getting ready to let out for the summer. The thread that held me together was the media arts program that I attended at Leave Out Violence. I had been invited to attend the Leadership Training Camp that was going to happen in August. All the youth who had been chosen were to be flown to Toronto, all expenses paid, then driven to the campsite in Haliburton. I was happy that I'd been selected but doubted that I would go.

Carma was still driving and loving me crazy. I managed to pass all of my classes despite wanting to quit school. As the white people made plans to go to their cottages for the summer and everyone I knew was making plans to party it up, Carma had other plans for me. I'd never really known God but I felt my soul leave me as my seventeen-year-old body sat slumped on the bathroom floor, leaning against the sink cabinet, crying. The tears came down my face and disgust was a hot, angry, jagged ball of wire in my chest. Carma had asked me to *work-work*. This time, it wasn't a solution to a problem — it was an ultimatum. He said that if it wasn't me then it would be someone else and we couldn't be together anymore.

I was hurt and confused. So many questions went through my mind. Why was this happening to me? Why would he say this to me? What was I going to do without him if I didn't comply? What other girl was he going to be with?

I thought of my dad. He was in jail. He didn't care about me. If he did, he wouldn't have gone back to jail and left me to fend for myself. The same went for my mom. She was around but I didn't care too much what she thought. If she cared, she wouldn't have kicked me out in the first place. Carma was all I had. I wasn't about to just hand him off to the next girl after everything we'd been through. I refused to do that. *He was mine* and I would do *anything* to keep it that way, even if it meant selling my body.

I thought about my body with all of its scars and lesions. I'd also been having a lot of trouble with my feet, and the nails on my big toes were painfully ingrown. I didn't know how that was going to work.

Carma had an answer for all of my questions and insecurities about working. He had given me the ultimatum and said that he would give me some time to think about it but I already had my answer.

"Well, how long would I have to do it?" I had asked.

"You get out what you put in; that all depends on *you*. I'm only trying to do this for a couple of years so we can have some money to get started with," he had replied.

Daneen came into the bathroom to see why I was crying. She must've heard me from her upstairs bedroom. I told her that Carma wanted me to work.

"Are you gonna do it?" she asked.

"Yeah, what other choice do I have?" I said.

"If you're gonna do it then why are you crying?" she asked.

It wasn't the ultimatum itself that was causing my tears.

"Do I just have to dance, like give guys lap dances?" I had asked Carma.

"Well, yeah. But dancers don't really make that much money anymore. You're eventually gonna have to do extras," he said.

I asked him if *extras* meant sex and stuff and he said yeah. "You want me to have sex for money?" I asked. I was in shock.

"It's not like you're a virgin. If you can do it for free then you can do it for money," he said.

I don't remember the full conversation but I remember the underlying factor being that we needed money. He had been selling weed and crack for a while but he didn't want to do that anymore.

Anyway, I would have done *anything* for Carma and he knew that. I finally had a way to pay him back for everything he had done for me. *It's time to grow up, Jade*, I told myself. I didn't feel like crying anymore. I was anxious to leave. I called him back and told him that I was down to do it.

Over the next few days, we hung out, driving around Dartmouth. Carma filled me in as best he could on what to expect.

"I need a name," I told him as we drove along Portland Street. From everything I'd seen on TV, strippers always had a fake name that was super sassy or sexually appealing.

He asked me what I wanted my name to be. "I don't know! You pick!" I said. I was curious to see what name he would come up with, how he would describe me.

He sat quiet in thought for a few minutes. "Spice," he said eventually.

"Spice," I repeated. "Why Spice?" I asked.

"That's what you make me think of," he said. "You're sweet and you have flavour but you always just have that little bit of extra kick, like a spice."

I laughed and agreed that Spice would be my name, repeating it to myself in my head.

We took the Greyhound bus to Montreal. I was still in the system, so I had to have some type of cover story. I lied to everyone except my closest girls and told them that I was going to visit Cammy in Toronto again and I gave the social worker Cammy's mom's contact information.

One of the first things I remember about that second trip to Montreal was the pampering I received. I got to get all prim and proper. I had everything I needed to look and feel beautiful. Carma's uncle escorted us all around town, showing us the best places to get everything done — hair, nails and outfits. The design on my nails was Versace, to match Carma's three-tone gold chain. My weave was long, flowing and perfectly blended. As they say, it was *slayed to the gods*! When we got to the store that sold heels for dancers, I was in awe! There were so many options to choose from! The store clerk showed us a wall that held shoes for beginners. I asked Carma to help me pick. His uncle kept saying that "we needed to go higher." That made me nervous. I wasn't used to wearing stiletto heels. I ended up going with a clear heel that had a white bottom. They had an ankle strap so they weren't *too* hard to walk in. Carma also bought me a brand new outfit — a pair of dark blue jeans with purple stitching and a matching purple shirt. It was a bit too tight for my liking but he said he loved it. He convinced me to put it on right away even though I hadn't had time to shower that morning, as his uncle was adamant about leaving the house first thing in the morning.

Once my looks were taken care of, we had to get an ID for me. We made a pit stop at a corner store that did passport-style photos. Carma's uncle had the hookup for fake IDs. After all, I was only seventeen, and you had to be at least eighteen to work in Montreal. The picture I took was so ugly but those guys said it didn't matter. Carma paid for everything and gave his uncle a few hundred dollars to pay for my ID, then we went back to his uncle's girl's house. Carma made supper while chatting with his uncle and I from where we sat at the table. His uncle called me out on my staring. "Why do you always look at me like that?" he asked.

"Like what?" I questioned back.

"Like you want a problem or something," he said with a short chuckle.

"Oh no, I just like to look at people when they're talking, ya know?" I said.

He never mentioned it again.

As I got ready to go to the club, Carma gave me a pep talk. He assured me that I would be fine. He quizzed me on the information on my fake ID. He made sure I knew to say my name was *Helena Thompson*. The only thing that changed on my birthday was the year I was born. I recited the fake address to him.

"Tonight is just practice, okay? Don't worry about making money, just make sure you practise talking to the customers, okay?" Carma said.

The whole time I was nodding my head to show that I understood while I put on sweet-smelling body lotion and spritzed myself with perfume. Before I left, I did a last-minute bag check to make sure I had my shoes, outfits and condoms. Then I kissed Carma, told him I loved him and followed his uncle's current girl, Barbie, to the waiting cab.

I managed to answer the questions from the bouncer and the owner with flirtatious ease. Barbie also worked her magic in persuading the owner that I was "good." I suppressed my nervousness up until I got in the door of the club.

Finally, we were in the dressing room. It was then that my nervousness set in. I suddenly felt sick. I was fidgeting with my hands when the owner came in and told us we had to go out on the floor. I rose to my feet and sauntered into the club like I'd practised, with my hips swaying and my heels barely leaving the floor. It gave the illusion that I was sort of gliding across the floor.

The bar seats were cold even though I sat on a bandana. This was what all of the girls did. The ones who made more money sat on brand-name scarves like Louis Vuitton and Gucci. I sat at the bar and observed the scene around me. There were coloured strobe lights illuminating the club and a stage with a single pole in the middle. As each girl did her stage show, I could see an array of personalities. Some danced slow and sexual and others danced very fast. The girls did crazy pole tricks and I wondered how in the hell they had learned to do them.

The bouncers stayed by the entrance, checking the IDs of the customers. There were quite a few men in the club but none of them approached me. All I got were a few glances as they looked over my nearly naked body from my feet to my face. I sported a black bikini with boy-short-style bottoms that showed more of my ass than they covered. The bikini top tied around my neck tightly and pushed my boobs up, creating cleavage that I didn't have.

Thankfully, I didn't have to do a stage show that night. I probably would've been frozen with fear. I was terrified and didn't speak to anyone all night. I worked myself into such a state of anxiety that I started to feel sick to my stomach again. I retreated to the dressing room where an older black girl sat doing her makeup. Soon after, a blonde-haired white chick stumbled in behind me. When she saw that I was feeling uneasy, she began talking to me.

"What's up? What's wrong? How old are you?" she asked, one question after another.

Tears sprang to my eyes. "I'm seventeen," I said.

The girl didn't even flinch at the fact that I was underage. She offered me a line of cocaine and told me it was easier when you had something to take the edge off, or something along those lines. Although I declined the offer, the black girl who had been touching up her makeup jumped to her feet. In an instant, she was nose to nose with the white girl. I couldn't place her accent but I knew that she was from somewhere in the Caribbean. She started yelling. "WHAT'S THE MATTA WITH YOU? DIDN'T YUH JUST 'EAR DI GYAL SAY SHE ONLY SEVENTEEN? HAVE YUH GONE MOD? GWAN FROM ROUND HERE!" she said. She proceeded to call the blonde girl names that mentioned her coke addiction.

I sat in my seat, speechless. The Caribbean woman made the white girl apologize to me before sending her back on the floor. I quietly thanked her afterward.

"Why are you here, honey? You're only seventeen," she said.

I shrugged my shoulders because I didn't know what to say. She pointed at my tattoo and asked if it was the name of my man. "No, it's my baby brother," I lied.

"All right," she said. She sighed and went out onto the floor. I started crying.

After a few minutes, Barbie came in. "What's wrong?" she asked, seemingly uninterested.

"Umm, my period is coming. I have cramps," I lied. I was told to sit tight until closing time. I got dressed and waited, not looking forward to the lecture Carma was probably going to give me. It was a good thing Carma didn't put a quota on me (meaning that I had to make a certain amount in one night) because I never would've made it. I made zero dollars that night.

To my surprise, the lecture never came. "It's okay. You did your best. Just try to get out there more next time, okay?" he said.

After that, Barbie began sending subliminal messages of her disapproval of me. I wasn't sure why. Before we moved to a different girl's house, Carma's uncle approached me. "Come take a walk with me," he said.

I was a bit nervous. I didn't really trust him. Not just because of his notorious past but because I'd heard that he was famous for knocking other pimps. This meant that he was known for "stealing" girls from their pimp, basically by convincing them to work for him instead. I didn't want to be put in that predicament.

As we walked, he gently took me by the arm and led me to the other side of the sidewalk — away from the street. "Why did you do that?" I asked him.

"A woman should never walk on the side closest to the street. A man is supposed to walk there. That way, if a car comes, it will hit me first and not you," he said.

In that moment, I forgot about all of the scary stories I'd heard and read about him. *Nobody has ever done that for me. Not even Carma*, I thought.

He spoke to me in a general way, issuing an apology on Barbie's behalf. "She's just mad 'cause I won't let her shop for the baby yet so she's taking it out on everyone," he said. I had wondered if she was pregnant but neither I nor Carma were sure. She looked like she had the beginning of a baby bump but I hadn't wanted to ask her.

It was as if Carma's uncle had known me forever or like I was part of the family. "Do you love Carma?" he asked. I told him I wouldn't be there if I didn't. "I can tell you two love each other, all you do is argue," he said, laughing.

I went back to that club once more. This time the manager told me to do a stage show. I was to pick three songs. By the end of the third song, I had to be topless. I stuck out like a dandelion in a bouquet of roses. I was called to the stage by my stripper name, *Spice.* The DJ announced my name in his radio personality voice like I was on the red carpet. I started out just walking around the stage, seductively, eyeing the crowd. I moved my body against the pole in an "S" movement. I tried to mimic the other girls' shows. I had been able to dance for years, grooving my body to the rhythm, so I did what I knew how. Where I was dancing to artists like Ciara and Rihanna, the other girls were dancing to country, French rap and techno.

I managed to get my first customer, who paid me $20 for one lap dance. I didn't really feel too much about it. It wasn't gross, weird or even particularly difficult. It was just what it was — a lap dance. I remember seeing Barbie dancing for a client through the half-closed curtain. Her belly was now swollen with child. I saw her pull a client's hands off of her stomach and wag her finger at him to say no, as one would do to a small child. It was uncomfortable to watch so I finished my dance and went back on the floor.

Carma and I were doing okay while I was there. We didn't have sex much but he cooked for me and we were together fairly often. He was also pretty playful with me, sometimes too much. Once we were wrestling and he got me in a choke hold. At first it was funny as I tried to wiggle my way out of his grip but then I really couldn't breathe.

"I can't breathe!" I wheezed. He must've thought I was joking because he didn't let go. "Seriously, Carma, I can't breathe," I tried again. Still — nothing.

Before I could try again, my body got tingly and I couldn't see anymore. When I came to, I was on the floor, cradled in Carma's arms. He was slapping me in the face to wake me up.

"What the hell?" I said. I was confused as to how I'd gotten on the floor. Barbie was standing in the doorway with her hand over her mouth.

"You passed out," Carma said.

"I told you I couldn't breathe, you idiot," I said to him.

"Oh my god, you girl, you were foaming at the mouth and everything," Barbie said.

"I swear you were having a seizure and all," Carma chimed in.

My cheeks grew hot with embarrassment. "That was scary. My eyes went black. Next time I say I can't breathe then let me go," I told him. He hugged me and let me go so that I could stand up. Barbie got me some water.

"Now what would you have done if I didn't wake up? Would you have flown my body home?" I asked.

"Yeah, of course but I didn't mean to," he said. He tried to hug me again but I told him I wasn't playing anymore. I knew that we had only been goofing around but how easily he was able to knock me out frightened me, even if it was by accident.

After a while at Barbie's house, I went to a different club with another one of Carma's uncle's girls whose name at the club was China. She was to be my mentor for the night. This club was in the country, on an old dirt road. It was pretty empty. There was porn playing on a big flat-screen TV fixed to the wall. It turned out China and another girl that worked there also worked for Carma's uncle. We didn't talk to her but I'd occasionally glance over at her to see what she was doing.

China let me have a drink with her as she coached me to talk to an old man who looked part corporate executive and part cowboy with his business attire and cowboy hat. She urged me to sit next to him, with my back straight like Carma had taught me on our first date, and put my hand on his thigh. I was to lean in close to his ear and ask him if he wanted to have some fun and go for a dance with me. I sat beside him but my words escaped me. China came to my rescue and introduced us as friends. While we were talking, she took my hand and placed it on his thigh without the man seeing. I was extremely uncomfortable and to be honest, I feared the rejection that I was sure would come, and it did. He didn't accept my invitation for a dance.

Pretty soon, I was over the whole scene, so I turned around in my bar stool and watched porn instead, asking myself why I ever bothered to start stripping. *It requires so much work just to get a man to go for a dance with you. I'm not a hustler like Barbie and China*, I thought.

Montreal was a bust. Even as a beginner, I knew I wasn't going to make any real money there. Carma agreed. And so, we left Montreal and went to Toronto in pursuit of a livelier scene where I could make some real money.

This time, we stayed on our own in a motel in Mississauga along Hurontario Street. I went to work at a club called Midway with a girl named Teegan. Teegan worked for Devin, one of Carma's best friends. Teegan was pretty cool for the most part. We chatted to guys together in the club. She had been working before me so she was better at it than I was, but it kind of worked because I was viewed as "the shy one" — which I was. Teegan was very outspoken and sexual with her "sales tactics." She would *tell* guys to take her for a dance instead of asking them to. A few times, she asked them if they wanted to come in the back and watch her eat my pussy or "go for a double" where the two of us would dance for one guy. I always blushed and we'd all laugh.

I bounced around to one or two more clubs. Teegan managed to get us into House of Lancaster — a popular strip club in downtown Toronto. The dancers were supposed to have a licence there but Teegan got me in anyway. I was nowhere near a pro pole dancer but I gained a bit more confidence and soaked up some knowledge from Teegan, so I was a bit more comfortable on stage at House of Lancaster than I was in Montreal.

There were three stages — the main one and two small, circular stages on the bar. I was told by the owner to go on one of the bar stages. I twisted and turned around the pole like I had all of the confidence in the world. Soon after, a really sexy black guy sat directly in front of my stage. In this lifestyle (also known as "the Game"), girls aren't allowed to service (have sexual interactions with) or even *talk* to black guys in the club. In fact, they're told to avoid eye contact at all by fixing their eyes on the floor if ever a black guy walked past them or was in their line of view. This was because another black man was seen as a threat, a potential contender to "take" your girl. I knew this. Everybody knew this. But I couldn't help myself. Although I knew I'd be deemed "out of pocket" (meaning I was not adhering to the rules of the game, thus being disrespectful), I decided to play with fire. I was afraid to imagine the consequences of my actions if Carma were to find out, so I pushed the thoughts from my head.

I didn't talk to him at first but we locked eyes for my entire show, which was typically three songs per set. I had no idea who he was but his eye contact was exciting and intimidating. He was dark-skinned and dressed in a business-casual type of style. I bounced myself up and down, directly in his face, standing up and shying away only when he cupped me in his hand.

When I came down onto the floor, he found me immediately. He asked to take me for a dance. I tried to sound casual. "Where are you from?" I asked.

"Montreal but I was born in Haiti," he replied with an accent I hadn't heard before. My interests were no longer sparked. Although I'd never met a Haitian man before, where I came from, they had a reputation for being violent. I'd heard stories of how they beat their women severely. I wasn't willing to play with fire any longer so I thanked him for watching my show and sauntered away. He grabbed my hand but I kept walking. I never saw him again.

Once the motel fees got to be too expensive, Carma moved us to where Teegan and her man Devin were staying at a house in Brampton. The house belonged to Devin's uncle, who was out of town at the time. The arguing between Carma and I had gotten really bad again. Every other day, I was being choked to the point where I could barely breathe. During one of our altercations, I was screaming so loudly, the neighbour called the police. When the police knocked on the door, Carma shook me and told me to shut the fuck up. "Do you want me to fucking go to jail?" he whispered viciously. Another stripper that was staying there with her man dealt with the police and told them that Carma and I were just drunk.

I refused to go to work a couple of times after that incident. Teegan continued to go to work and see her regulars outside of work, either before her shift or on her days "off." Carma and Devin were gone a lot. When we weren't at work, Teegan and I were usually alone. We formulated a plan to keep some of our money hidden from the boys, just in case. In case of what, I didn't know. We never followed through with it though, whatever it might have been.

I think Teegan ended up telling Devin about hiding the money. I think he blamed me for the whole thing because he never liked me much. He tolerated me, at most. I didn't like him either but we were respectful of one another to some capacity. In Brampton, we went on a double date. The guys treated us to dinner at the Keg. The bill was outrageous: it was over $200 for the four of us. Carma and Devin paid. When we got back to the house, three of us were stuffed and constipated, except for Carma who found it hilarious. It ended up being a night in for all of us.

Somehow, after dinner, Carma, Teegan and I got on the topic of a foursome. Devin was gone off in another part of the huge house. All I did was laugh at the idea. I couldn't imagine having sex with Teegan's boyfriend. He was sexy but I had no desire toward him.

Teegan had long since said she was bisexual. "I already told Jade I would eat her pussy. I wasn't joking," she told Carma.

"Show me!" Carma teased.

I was just about to get in the shower before Teegan showed both of us just how serious she was. She ripped off my towel and pushed me onto the bed with Carma sitting there beside us. I burst out laughing. "Umm, no!" I said.

She didn't let up. Instead, she told Carma to hold my arms as she pried my legs apart and got between them. I resisted at first, trying to squirm out of her grasp but she knew what she was doing so I stopped fidgeting and put my hands in her hair. Just as we got somewhat comfortable, Carma jumped up and left the room. Teegan continued for another minute or two. When she finished, I wrapped the towel back around me, blushing.

Carma brought Devin into the room. "Teegan, you cheated on me with Jade?" he asked. We all laughed.

They left the room and it was just me and Carma. "Why did you leave?" I asked. I told him that I'd only done it so that he could watch.

"I thought you guys might want some privacy for the first time," he said as he smirked.

I started laughing. "You're stupid," I said.

Suddenly, Teegan burst back into the room and told me to tell Carma how she had made me moan. "Her hands were in my hair and all!" she said loudly. My cheeks were burning with embarrassment so I ditched them and headed to the shower.

It was around this time that the pain in my feet became too much to bear. It got so bad that I had to go to the emergency room to get my toenail removed. It was still growing in crooked, causing a lot of pressure on my foot and discolouration around my nail.

Carma and I hopped (me, literally, and in tears) into a cab accompanied by Teegan who was letting me use her health card, since I didn't have mine with me in Toronto. Once there, we sat together in the waiting room and waited for Teegan's name to be called. Finally, they called her name and I went to get assessed. After telling the lady my problem, I hobbled back to where Teegan and Carma were sitting, stifling their laughter. "What's so funny?" I asked.

I can't remember their exact response but it sounded very suspicious. I half laughed with them, saying, "Shut up! You're saying it like you two had sex."

The two of them stopped laughing and got quiet. I reeled my head around to look at the two of them. My jaw dropped. "YOU GUYS FUCKED?" I asked loudly.

Carma told me to be quiet as they tried to explain themselves, claiming that it had been a one-time thing, long before Teegan was with Devin and even longer before Carma had met me. Devin had known and didn't care. I looked at them in disbelief, feeling stupid and betrayed for having been kept in the dark. I started crying and moved away from them, sitting alone. When I finally went in to see the doctor I was still in tears and Carma asked if I wanted him to come with me. I gave him a death stare and said, "No," but he followed me anyway. I ignored anything he had to say, unable to control my crying.

The doctor went over the procedure and gave me a local anesthetic through two needles in my toe. He left, giving the anesthetic time to numb the surgical area. I continued to ignore Carma when he asked if I could still feel anything.

When the doctor returned and tapped on my foot to check my progress, I cried out in pain. I'm not sure if it was because I was so worked up or if I had a high tolerance to the anesthetic but I could still feel the pain, even after the doctor applied another dosage. Apologizing, he said that he couldn't inject any more freezing and that he would have to go ahead with the procedure anyway.

With me crying hysterically, he began. First, he shoved a clamp-like surgical tool all the way under my nail, down to the cuticle, then he began snipping away at the piece of nail that was embedded in my skin. It was so painful — I thought I was going to throw up and pass out. Before he could do the other side of my toenail, he asked Carma to help by holding me still. This added anger to my pain, though the doctor didn't know what he had just caused.

"Don't touch me!" I said repeatedly.

"You have to get this done so I need to hold you still. You're gonna feel so much better afterward," Carma said as he stroked my hair and put his body weight on my torso.

After what seemed like an eternity of torture, the procedure was over and I was allowed to leave. I had to sit in a wheel-chair because of the state of my foot. I had no other choice but to let Carma push me. When the cab came, I tried to haul myself out of the wheelchair with little success. I was in a lot of pain and exhausted from crying. Carma lifted me into his arms, like a child, into the cab and then into the house. All the while, I was crying, telling him to put me down. By the time we got back to the house, I was ready for bed and to give Carma and Teegan the silent treatment for a little while.

As annoying as it was, Carma and I moved yet again. We were steadily packing and unpacking. With all of the moving around in foster homes and now this, I was used to leaving at a moment's notice. This time, we went to a condo in Mississauga to stay with another one of Carma's friends who was in the Game. His name was Silas.

We probably had the most fun there with Silas. Carma took me on more dates with other couples where we went out to eat and bowling and things like that. I'm a pretty good bowler too. I remember the guys placing bets on whose girlfriend was best. I'm pretty sure I won. I mean, I had to have. Carma was cheering for me the whole time and whenever I got a low score he would say things like, "Oh no! I thought I could count on you!"

At one point, Silas had to leave the city so Carma and I got to drive around in Silas's brand new black Mustang, even though he had given us clear instructions to drive his older car. It felt like we were a rich couple during that time.

As had been the case before, another girl took me under her wing and brought me to the club where she worked. This time, it was Silas's girl, Alexis, a white girl from Montreal.

I don't remember the name of the club, but it was there that I did my first "extra" in the VIP room. At this club, the private dance section was downstairs instead of off to the side on the main floor like the other clubs I had been at. It was technically illegal to perform sexual services in strip clubs but everyone was doing it on the down low. Did the managers know about it? Of course they did, but it brought in more business. Sometimes, in addition to tipping the DJ or paying the manager to work at the club, girls would slip him a little extra cash to keep his mouth shut about what they were doing.

My first customer was a pot-bellied white man. He offered to pay me $60 for a blowjob. I wasn't too sure of the price rules and it was my first offer, so I agreed. We went to the VIP room. He sat in an old armchair and a thin curtain was the only thing that shielded us from the rest of the girls and customers. I got down on my knees on the cold floor and pulled a condom from my purse. Rolling it onto him, it was over almost as quickly as it began. Within five minutes, he finished and I was $60 richer. I rose to a standing position.

"Thanks! That was great!" he said with much enthusiasm. I smiled. In my mind, it was the easiest $60 I'd ever made. I tried but failed to make the calculations of how much money I could've made if I'd charged the same price for every blowjob I'd ever given in my personal life. I snapped out of it and headed back to the main floor.

Although I began to make a bit of money, Carma and I still couldn't avoid the heated arguments. It seemed like nothing I did could make him happy. He was never satisfied. When I listened, he claimed I could be doing more. When I didn't listen, it was a screaming match and he was choking the shit out of me.

He didn't tell me I had to make a certain amount of money each night. But he would ask how much I made and then I would hand over all of the money to his waiting hands. When he counted my earnings, he asked me for a rundown of what I'd done that night and what I'd charged. Five measly dollars was unaccounted for and I had some change in there too. I'd bought a drink but I didn't want to tell him that because I wasn't allowed to be drinking, so I told him I didn't know.

"Maybe I dropped something," I said.

He started yelling at me. "Pay better attention to your money before you get robbed!"

It was around then that I was having problems with my foot again. With the trip to the hospital and all of the arguing we were doing, Carma decided that it was time for us to go home. He told me I was costing him too much money and that he *loved me too much* to keep doing this with me.

It was August by then, a week shy of the start date for LOVE's Leadership Training Camp. Initially, I had to decline the offer because I was away with Carma. But seeing as how we were going home, I decided to try my luck and ask the Executive Director if the offer still stood. To my surprise, someone had dropped out at the last minute and so there was space for me. I asked Carma if I could go, and he gave me permission to attend.

CHAPTER 10

GOING BACK

The experience at camp was phenomenal. At first, I kept my phone on me and mostly hung out with Jordan. I was really shy and there were tons of youths from other regions all across the country — Toronto, Montreal, Vancouver, even New York. I didn't know who to talk to outside of Jordan.

Within a day or two, my phone was put away and I came out of my shell. I took a workshop called "The F Word" that talked about forgiveness. That workshop was one of the things that began to help me realize how much I actually needed to break up with Carma. Out of all the love that flowed through each youth leader and staff member, I began to realize that what I had with Carma was not love. The realization made me feel horrible, yet I found strength in it too.

An activity in the workshop instructed us to write a letter to someone, asking for forgiveness or forgiving someone else. I wrote a letter to Carma, forgiving him for all that we'd been through. We were invited to read our letters aloud but I never did. I ended up burning it in the campfire sometime that week. Another memorable activity we did was write something that we'd like to let go of on rocks before we took turns throwing them off the gazebo, into the lake. I'd written Carma's name on my rock and hurled it at the water.

I'd done it. I'd gotten all of my thoughts and feelings out of my head and onto paper. The lake rock symbolized my closure. I was finally ready to let go.

Or so I thought.

Toward the end of camp, there was talk of momentum and how we must not let it fade once we got back home. I didn't know what they meant. I was charged up! I felt happy! I was *sure* I could maintain my newfound strength. I told myself I was going to break up with Carma when I got back. It felt good. I felt empowered. This was not the *love* that I wanted.

That was all good until I got home. The momentum did fade, along with my strength to leave. I no longer had my new friends around me. I'd forgotten what I'd written in the letter before it was burned. My lake rock was now just another among many on the bottom of the lake. I was on my own again and so I went home to Carma and pushed away any thought of a breakup ever happening. Besides, when I got back, the familiarity in his eyes and the comfort of his presence was enough to remind me that this was the man I loved. This was the man I would do anything for. The one I would put my life on the line for.

School started back up. Carma and I returned for our grade twelve year. I was really confused as to where we stood in terms of our relationship, but I loved him all the same. He was seeing at least four other girls in addition to me. We continued to argue about their presence in his life. He argued that they were giving him money. I told him that they were unnecessary.

"You know you're my woman and I know you're my woman and *my mom* knows you're my woman so I don't really care what anyone else thinks," he said.

I still hated it and I continued to tell him so. I had girls messaging me telling me that they were in a relationship with him. I had outsiders messaging me saying, "Isn't Carma your man? I heard he talks to so and so." It drove me crazy! I masked my frustration and anger by seeming confident in my relationship and completely unbothered by the girls who claimed that Carma was *their* man. One girl even messaged me on Facebook wishing me a happy birthday. I politely thanked her then asked her not to contact me anymore for any reason. Apparently Carma had sent her an *I love you too* text message!

It seemed like all these girls were trying to do was throw it in my face that they were involved with Carma. It was as if they were trying to spite me. Carma had taken this one girl to Applebee's for her birthday and bought her flowers. Immediately, she blasted it on Facebook. When someone told me about the post, I was in a rage! *Anybody but her!* I thought. This girl had a *terrible* reputation and it was rumored that she had an STI called trichomoniasis. I hadn't even heard of that before! Usually people caught chlamydia or even herpes but trichomoniasis was something new. I lost my mind wondering if they were having sex.

I was damned if she had one up on me but she did. *My man* had spent his money and energy ensuring that she had a special birthday. I was furious at him but mostly embarrassed for myself because I knew other people knew about it being blasted on Facebook. That night, with no exaggeration whatsoever, I called Carma's phone more than fifty times in a row. He hung up on me the first two times and then let it ring every other time until eventually his line went straight to voicemail. I bawled harder each time he didn't answer, until I couldn't breathe.

The next day, when he finally did call back, he ignored my questions about his whereabouts the previous night. Instead, he laughed at me and told me I was crazy.

I was spent — exhausted from crying and tired of him treating me how he was treating me. "Do you know what it's like to have someone tell you that the one you love is out on a date with someone else?" I sobbed.

"I don't care what anyone else has to say. If you're mad, step your game up! That girl just gave me money so I took her out. It's not that serious," he said.

But it was to me. I figured there was no use in crying so I thought about how I could "step my game up."

*　*　*

That June, I graduated from high school. All of my family was in attendance. Jordan, Laila and Daneen were also graduating so their family members were there too. From my seat, in my cap and gown, I scanned the crowd for Carma. He was not there. I checked my phone again. He said he was on his way but *where was he*, I wondered. I got anxious as the names of the people in my graduating class were called. My eyes welled up with tears at the realization that he was not going to make it. A text from him confirmed my thoughts. He wasn't going to make it. Once I knew that, I let the tears fall freely from my eyes.

I had waited for this moment for three long years, to graduate high school, and all I wanted was the love of my life to see me do it. Instantly, the last three years of school that I'd struggled through did not matter anymore. It didn't matter that my siblings were there or that my parents were there waiting to rush to the stage to photograph me. Without Carma there, nothing mattered. Jordan's mom made eye contact with me from across the aisle. "Are you okay?" she whispered, probably alarmed at my state of emotion. I shook my head and looked away.

"Jade Brooks," someone called from the stage. I slowly walked up to where some of my teachers and the school principal stood. Someone made a little speech about me, announcing that I had received a $2,500 scholarship to college and that I had made the honour roll. These were details I received after the ceremony from my mom. I didn't hear any of it.

When I got off the stage, my family came to give me a hug and congratulate me. I was crying even harder now. "Look, she's so happy she's crying!" my mom said. Meghan saw something else in my demeanor. "What's wrong?" she asked.

I choked on the words as I tried to relay them. "Carma's not here," I said, having to repeat it a couple of times. When Quin came up to me to ask for a photo op, I hugged her and asked if anyone clapped for me. "Yeah, what do you mean?" she asked. She didn't understand how I hadn't heard the thunder of applause.

After the ceremony, Carma finally made it. When I came outside, he was standing there with a gift bag in his hand. He smiled his big smile and I started crying again. "You missed it," I said.

"I'm sorry, baby. I got lost. I didn't know where it was. I got you something," he replied.

I blinked back tears as he handed me the gift bag. I looked at him, standing there with his sharp outfit. His smile eased me. I opened the bag. There was a congratulatory card inside. With his messy writing, he had written, *Congratulations* and signed it with, *Love Carma xoxo*. I pulled a long box out of the bag and looked at Carma again. "What is this?" I laughed nervously.

"Open it," he said.

The blush in my cheeks was making my face hurt. After taking the wrapping paper off the box, I pulled out a gold chain. Tears sprang to my eyes. Carma slipped the chain from my hands and told me to turn around so that he could put it on me. I lifted my hair from my neck and looked down as the chain fell fairly heavy on my chest.

"I'm so proud of you," he said.

I turned around and gripped him in a bear hug. "Thank you, baby doll," I said. I was happy but I couldn't shake the heart-rending feeling that I had about him missing the ceremony.

In regards to "stepping my game up," I barely had a chance to even begin to execute a plan, because a few days later Carma came to see me and told me that he had another girl who was willing to go work for him in Toronto. It turned out there was a girl from his school that he'd been seeing for quite some time. She was a white girl that I'd never heard of before.

"What's her name?" I asked.

"Alyssa," he said.

Cadence, who went to the neighbouring school near Carma's, told me that she knew of this Alyssa but didn't know her personally. Although I didn't know her either, I hated her. Not only was she trying to steal my man from me, she was white! That felt like a slap in the face. None of the other girls he had been talking to were white. *What's so special about her?* I asked myself constantly. That summer, Carma flew to Toronto with her and without me.

To my knowledge, I was still his girlfriend. He planned to be gone for the month of July. I tried not to start any arguments between us but I couldn't help it. I was so sad; I felt abandoned.

"Where's Alyssa?" I always asked him.

"You seem more worried about her than me," he'd say.

When I got to be too annoying for him, he would threaten to hang up on me.

While Carma was gone, his mom invited me to their family reunion. I was reluctant to accept the invitation since Carma wasn't going to be there, but eventually decided I would go. The reunion was jam-packed with food, drinks, tents, plastic chairs and relatives in matching t-shirts. I found Carma's mom and joined her where she sat with her sisters and cousins. I was told to help myself to the food. As I stood eating homemade dinner rolls, one of Carma's aunties came over to me.

"You're Carma's girlfriend, ain't ya? I saw your tattoo," she said.

I smiled but immediately regretted wearing shorts and exposing his name inked deep into the flesh on my thigh. I didn't like being put on the spot. I knew the others were watching and listening.

"Didn't Carma leave you and move to Toronto with that girl?" she asked, rather obnoxiously.

I kept my composure, laughing with the others. "He's coming back!" I insisted.

"You're some stupid. I wouldn't be letting my man go nowhere with no girl. And that tattoo . . . I tell ya, the young girls today . . ." she said, her sentence drifting off. I thought she would never stop. I felt stupid.

Thankfully, Carma's mom came through and asked me to take her granddaughter back to the house to use the bathroom. "Just stay there. I'll be right behind you," his mom said. When she came, I expressed my embarrassment and she told me not to worry about the aunt. "That woman ain't got no manners," she said. I brushed it off as best I could.

When Carma and I weren't arguing, we found comfort in sending each other nude pictures and videos. If there was one thing we never lacked, it was sexual chemistry. I'd send him pictures of me in a thong or booty shorts and he'd send me clips of himself jerking off. I always told him how much I missed him and sometimes he'd let me know that he missed me too. We'd do this whenever *she* wasn't around. Sometimes she would be in another room of the house or gone out doing whatever and if it was night time, she was at work.

I asked him if they had sex and he said if she had a good night or something to that degree. He went on to say that if she wasn't making any real money then she didn't deserve to have sex with him just for the sake of it. Somehow, I was satisfied with this response. Whatever it was, I couldn't wait to be near him again.

Toward the end of the month, Carma asked if I would come back to Toronto to work. "I *need* you to come through for me this time," he said.

I noted how strongly he'd emphasized the word *need*. "Where's Alyssa?" I asked him.

"She left," Carma replied.

I felt smug. Like every other girl, I'd known she wouldn't last and I took the opportunity to tell him that.

"You're so right. I see that now. Just come. It'll be just me and you this time, I promise," he said.

I believed that it would be and so I agreed to come back on one condition: "We have to have one weekend of fun, just us," I said. He promised to make it happen and then booked my flight without hesitation.

Back in Toronto for the second time, Carma kept his promise. We drove to Niagara Falls for the weekend. We had a blast! Carma asked the ticket booth attendant at the Clifton Hill attractions which of the haunted houses was the scariest and we went to that one. It didn't disappoint. I had my eyes shut tight almost the entire time. I was so scared that my whole body was tense and I clung to Carma as we walked. When a picture was snapped of us inside the house, the expression on Carma's face was hilarious! As for me, my head was ducked under his arm. We took dozens of pictures, outside of the house, on a disposable camera and he had them developed for me.

When we went on a ride that carried you slowly to the top then dropped you *really* fast, I dropped my sandal and screamed all the way down. Scenes from the movie *Final Destination* flashed through my mind. Even Carma was scared! But my favourite, and probably his too, was the Ferris wheel. When the Ferris wheel stopped at its highest point, I kissed Carma really hard. Right away, he was rock hard. Leave it to us to get horny on a damn ride! I told him to pull his pants down some and gave him head right there on the top of the wheel. He laughed but allowed me to do my thing, calling me a freak. I just wanted to show him how much I'd missed him. I stopped when we started moving again and repeated the gesture a couple of times before the ride was over.

Too soon, the weekend came to an end. He told me he had spent somewhere around $3,000 on a hotel, food and Clifton Hill. We headed back to Toronto — back to business.

I got another one of his pep talks. This time, he had a "no bullshit" approach. "I can't be arguing with you all the time. I need you to focus. Fuck everyone else. We're gonna do it right this time. It's you and me against the world," he said.

I kissed his hand, wrapping it in mine and said, "Okay." We recited our little mantra — "Shawty get it in but Daddy go hard!" I think he got it from a Jay-Z song or something.

Carma had me — mind, body and soul — and that's what he had said he wanted. This time, I was prepared to do anything I could to show him that he'd made the right decision by choosing me again.

This time around I wasn't going to be working in a strip club — I would be working at a massage parlour. The parlour was a full service, erotic spa where "everything goes." It was there that sex with clients became the norm for me. I saw clients from every race and walk of life. Some were all-American white boys out for a good night and some would spend a lot of the session sniffing lines of coke. There were middle-aged men, a lot of businessmen and I had one Somalian client come in on his eighteenth birthday (he said he wasn't a virgin, but I'm not sure I believed him). Some clients wanted to get straight to the point and others were more interesting or required the type of session where we would talk about their wives, jobs and whatever.

Men selected the girl they wanted. Our madam — a short lady with a strong stature — paraded the half-naked ladies into the room for an expecting customer. One time, the man quickly told the madam that he wanted to see me. I made my way over to him carefully, so as not to stumble in my heels, and smiled at him with a practised shyness. The madam whispered to me, urgently explaining that the customer wanted to do an outcall — my first outcall. I looked at her, expressionless, but nodded in agreement.

I followed him out to the cab reluctantly, attempting to make small talk and be flirtatious. While doing so, I was texting the cab driver's information to Carma from the placard on the back of the car seat. I was wondering, *How is Carma okay with this? This is dangerous!* It worried me how much trust our madam had in a stranger. Being new to the city, I had no idea where I was going. I tried to remember street names as we ventured further and further away from the massage parlour.

We pulled up to his house, walked around to the side door and went in. He encouraged me to sit down while he went to freshen up. His house was basic and dreary, with bland-coloured furniture and no paint on the walls. Just as I had the idea to grab his address from a piece of mail on the table, he came back into the room. I panicked a little inside but tried to smother the feeling. I prayed silently and vowed I would never do another outcall again.

I took my clothes off and kept on only the tiny bikini that barely covered my nipples. I slid back into my heels. I broke into character, going through the motions of dealing with a client. Smile. Laugh. Brush his leg sheepishly. I leaned in close enough for him to smell the candy-like fragrance I was wearing. When he kissed my neck, I slid away from him and stood — I was disgusted, but I made the gesture seem teasing. I reached in my purse for a condom and saw his excitement through his pants as he led me to his room.

A part of me was so disgusted that I wanted to gag, but before I knew it, I was on the verge of an orgasm. *Was I actually enjoying this?* I almost wanted to welcome it but at the same time it felt so wrong. I was so embarrassed when I came. "I was good? Yes?" he asked with a heavy European accent. I can't remember my response. I dressed silently and hurried into a cab. I beat myself up inside my head all the way back to work and while I was with other clients that night.

At the end of my shift, when our madam finally pulled up outside of the condo I was staying at with Carma and Silas's girl, I was more than thankful as I scurried inside. I fumbled in my bag for my cellphone. I had to call Carma to come downstairs and let me in.

Dropping my bag and flinging my shoes aside, I angrily undressed and headed to the shower. Carma followed me, asking what was wrong. Calmly, but sternly, I said, "Never make me do that again," and shut the door.

While the hot water poured over me it felt more like liquid hatred. I couldn't believe what had just happened. By the time I mustered up the energy to get out and face him again, I was still smothering a feeling of panic. I felt like I had just cheated on him and it was written all over my face — a feeling ten times worse than the one I'd had earlier that night when I didn't know the exact address of where I was going. If anyone, especially another girl from the spa, found out what I'd done, what I'd allowed to happen, I'd never be able to show my face again.

I climbed into bed beside Carma and he lifted his arm up, beckoning for me to lay my head on his chest — a place where, normally, I would have found solace. I refused him and turned my back toward him in a way that said leave me alone. I curled up within myself and hoped he would let it go but, of course, he wasn't the type of guy you could say no to. He grabbed my arm and turned me back toward him.

He tried to console me again by asking what was wrong but his tone was half curious and half annoyed. "What happened?" he asked.

I burst into tears and repeated that it wasn't my fault.

"What isn't your fault?" he asked. I began to tell him, through sobs, how the customer made me orgasm. I was too embarrassed to even look at him and see his expression. I hoped he would choose his words carefully before reassuring me that it wasn't my fault. "Your body simply reacted to the stimulation. It doesn't mean you were aroused by the man," Carma said.

I hugged him tighter than I could explain in words and apologized for letting it get to that. I couldn't sleep until I let him know that my body, my love and those special moments were his alone. He accepted my apology and told me that he already knew.

But did he really? Again, I forced myself to push the questions to the back of my mind but I couldn't help but wonder if I was built for this. I was still wrapped around him, as if letting him go would mean that I'd breathe no more. Something inside of me said, "No, Jade, this is not for you." Without exploring the thought any further I drifted into sleep, because come 5 o'clock I knew I'd be right back at it.

I made pretty good money at the spa most of the time. It was there that I made my first $1,000 in one night. But it wasn't good enough. That night, Carma and I argued about something or other and I threw a fist full of money in his face. "Take it!" I yelled at him. I told him again that money didn't mean anything to me. His hands gripped my throat for the trillionth time. This time, Silas's girl came rushing out of her room. I thought she was coming to help me but she ran out of the front door instead while I cried and struggled to breathe.

When things calmed down, Carma made me pick up every bill and place each one in his hand. I took out my phone and saw that I had received a text from the girl saying, *Sorry girl, I really wanted to help you but I can't. Si would've fucked me up for getting in the middle of it. Hope you understand! Take care girl xoxox.*

I replied by saying that I understood. It was fucked up but I truly did understand. I probably would've done the same thing. The girl was generally sweet. Sometimes she cooked a healthy breakfast for all of us with turkey bacon, egg whites and whole-wheat toast. When I overheard Silas telling Carma that she had cancer and received weekly treatments, I felt worse for her than I did for myself. He said she was a "crazy hood bitch" who had wanted to "get down with him from jump" (meaning that she wanted to be with him from the very beginning), so he let her. I didn't think it was right for her to be a prostitute when she was practically dying, but who was I to say anything?

I rotated through a couple of spas around the GTA. For the most part, when I serviced my clients, I wasn't mentally there. As I lay beneath them, they stopped being people and started being a blurred stream of faces. It wasn't like on TV and movies when women "go to their happy place." I didn't go anywhere. I just wasn't there.

Some clients were polite and others were very rough with me and disrespectful. I remember forgetting to get my money first from one young client, and he tried to leave without paying. I hated to start a commotion but I couldn't let him go, free of charge, after having had sex with me. Before he could get out the front door, five other girls pounced on him and restrained him until he agreed to pay me. It was so embarrassing. A couple of them asked why I didn't get the money first.

"I wasn't thinking," I said sheepishly.

"Purse first, ass last!" someone said, reciting one of the oldest rules in the industry.

You should've known better, I berated myself. Truthfully, I had just been tired and inattentive. I don't know what would have happened if the other girls hadn't been there.

In the spa business, the attendants are supposed to carry special licences deeming them able to carry out their job. I had been working toward getting one but I never got around to doing so. The madam even had a system where girls could work to pay for their licence and she would hold the money for them until they had enough. She also offered to drive girls to the licence office. There were a few other girls who weren't licensed either. If we were caught working without a licence, we could be criminally charged and the madam could face a fine and/or have her business shut down. So she would remind us about this cue in case the cops came into the spa. We'd listened to her little talks but I never really paid much attention to them. *What are the odds of a cop coming in to check licences?* I'd think to myself. But sure enough, one night, that cue — I think it was a trick with the light — came without warning and the unlicensed girls, including me, had to run out the back door of the spa. All at once, five or six half-naked girls in high heels ran out to the back parking lot and ducked between the cars in the dark. I was out of breath from running but my adrenaline was pumping from the thought of getting caught. I pulled my robe around me to lessen the chills I had from being outside in a bikini. When the cops checked the licences and left, we were admitted back into the spa and everyone went back to their normal routine.

One night after work, I smoked a blunt while waiting for our driver. Of course, I texted Carma and got permission from him first but it was still a bad idea. I was high out of my eighteen-year-old mind. Since I had stopped smoking weed back when Carma first told me to, I couldn't control my thoughts anymore when I was high.

It began to hit me that I was a prostitute and I was prostituting for Carma. I started to panic on the inside, realizing that I was not in a good place. *How did I get here?* I asked myself. It seemed like forever before the driver dropped us all off. I got back to the condo around 8 or 8:30 a.m. Our shift had been from 5 p.m. to 7 a.m. I was the last girl to get dropped off. I called Carma to come downstairs and let me in.

"You're fried, ain't ya?" he asked.

"Shut up," I said.

I wasn't my usual giddy, high self. There was anger in the back of my throat, threatening to explode in a slur of insults toward Carma. I went straight to the shower to try to bring my high down. When I finished, he was asleep. I crawled into bed beside him and watched him sleep, thinking absurd and violent thoughts, thinking I could kill him.

He woke up to see me lying on my side, staring at him.

"What are you looking at?" he asked. In his face, it looked like he knew what I was doing. "The devil is right in you right now," he said.

I started crying. My thoughts had frightened me. I was even more afraid when he called me out on it. Still high, I admitted to him that I was thinking about killing him.

He asked me how I would've done it.

"I was picturing me smothering you with the pillow," I told him.

"Stop crying. I know you wouldn't have done it. No more smoking," he said.

I was able to stop crying but my insecurities vocalized themselves. "Do you still love me even though I have sex for money?" I asked.

"Of course I do. I love you even more because you're doing it to better us," he said.

"Do I feel looser now?" I asked, referring to my vagina. I worried that having all that sex with customers made our sex less enjoyable for him.

"It feels the same to me," he replied.

I didn't want to go to sleep because I was too high so I asked him to make love to me instead, and he did.

After I had worked at the spa for a little longer, our arguing had reached new heights. But now, it was Carma who was fed up with *me*.

"Put your shoes on, we're going for a walk," he said.

I followed him out the door and into the elevator. The two of us were quiet for a while. We walked around the grounds of the condo. It was late at night. The grounds were well kept. It was chilly outside but not too cold.

Carma broke the silence first. "I can't do this with you anymore. We argue too much," he said.

"What do *you* mean you can't do *this*?" I asked, emphasizing my words.

"This isn't gonna work. All we do is argue with each other. I love you too much. I want us to go home," he said.

Instead of being relieved, especially after the breakdown

I'd had while high, I didn't want to go home! *I can do this! We can do this!* I thought. I dreaded the thought of us breaking up. I felt like he was abandoning our relationship and abandoning me, like he was walking out on everything we had built and were trying to build. I was hopeful that he would change his mind.

"Are you sure?" I asked him.

He said he was. My hope quickly turned to anger. *How dare he say he doesn't want to do this with me after everything I've done for us? After all that I've endured, he has the audacity to tell me that he wants to go home*, I thought furiously.

"Carma, if we go home this time, I'm not coming back. I'm not working anymore if we go home. Are you sure?" I asked again.

"I'm sure. I don't want to have to fight with you all the time. I love you too much," he said.

"Fine," I replied and stomped off toward the condo.

And just like that, we were back in Nova Scotia as if none of it had happened.

CHAPTER 11

HOME AGAIN

Carma and I agreed that each of us would attend college. I applied to the Office Administration program at Nova Scotia Community College in Halifax and got accepted at the last minute. I used the bursary that I received when I graduated high school for my first year tuition, even though my plans for attending any type of post-secondary schooling had been halted by Carma and I going to Toronto. Carma had received a similar bursary so he applied to the Business Administration program at the same community college in the Dartmouth location. He wanted to be a business owner, so I thought it only made sense for me to learn all of the admin side of business so that I could be his secretary and help him run his business.

I dove into school headfirst. I put everything that had happened over the summer in the back of my mind. At first,

I was mad at Carma for saying he didn't want to be in the Game with me but then I was happy to be done with it all. Maybe we shouldn't have done it in the first place, but at least he loved me enough to put a stop to it. I was happy to be home and to be in school. This way, Carma and I could do things the *right* way by focusing on our studies and graduating. We had every intention to pursue the family and lifestyle we had talked about except it would take us longer than initially anticipated, since we weren't getting that fast money anymore. We were chasing the dream!

School was good in the beginning, but as fall changed into winter, I began to lose focus. The cold weather had always been (and still is) difficult for me; it made me depressed. I didn't study and my assignments were piling up. I began to hate my classes. Who knew being a secretary was so hard? There were aspects of arranging things in alphabetical order that I was completely unaware of! I began to wonder if it was worth the stress and contemplated talking to Carma about going back to work at the massage parlour. I had a feeling that he wouldn't be in favour of it.

I told him about wanting to quit school.

"You don't want to work. You don't want to go to school. What do you want to do?" he asked.

We got into an argument about it because I said that I didn't know what I wanted to do. I just wanted to love him and have him love me back. I wanted him to make my decision for me, to tell me what I should do. That was what I was used to — him being my motivator, telling me which jobs to accept and when to quit them, what to say to club and spa owners, how to talk to customers, everything. He was everything to me; I didn't want to be left to make the decision for myself. I was working at Tim Hortons at the time but Tim's wasn't going to pay me enough to survive on my own, let alone take care of me and Carma. And so, I had a decision to make.

On Christmas break, two things happened. The first was that I quit school. I didn't have the mental capacity for it. Academically, I was fully capable but between the course load, teachers and going back and forth with Carma, I was losing my mind. I felt sick all the time. When I should've been studying for exams, I was sleeping to avoid reality. It was a struggle just to stay awake. The stress of it all was exhausting me. I hated everyone and everything. I was always irritated and ended up arguing with my teacher about my final accounting exam, which I ended up failing. I needed more time to study, but she was unmoved by my request to rewrite the exam at a later date. *Great!* I thought sarcastically.

To make matters worse, I found out I was pregnant . . . again.

It turned out all of the irritability and fatigue were symptoms of pregnancy. In fact, the sickness wasn't sickness at all but *nausea*. It wasn't a coincidence that the smell of Tim Hortons coffee in the morning was now disgusting me, it was the baby. I had been taking a birth control pill called Tricyclen, but I'd missed a few. Carma was familiar with the way the birth control worked. He would tell me to take two the next day but we continued to have sex with no protection as we'd always done, even when I was working at the massage parlour. After missing so many, I eventually stopped taking them altogether. We discussed that and agreed to start being more careful, but we never were. Everything we did was without a condom. I guess I hadn't been paying attention to my body at the time, with everything that was going on, because I didn't notice that I'd missed my period at first.

It was weird because his mom had asked me if I was pregnant. "Your nose is getting some wide!" she added. I lied and told her that I wasn't pregnant.

The first time I was pregnant, I had no symptoms at all. This pregnancy was different. Plus, I was no longer that fifteen-year-old girl whose mommy made her major life decisions for her. I was eighteen and approaching adulthood. This time around, the decision was mine to make. Still, I knew I had to speak to Carma about it. I daydreamed about his reaction to my announcement. I imagined he would initially be shocked and upset but that he would accept the fact that we were entering the next phase of our relationship — being parents. I mean, we'd already been through so much together, for so long; having a baby together was the next natural step — or so I thought.

I was only partially correct in guessing what his reaction would be. He *was* shocked. But then he asked me questions about my period and birth control, accusing me of not taking it on purpose. This was obviously not true. I had forgotten sometimes but I wasn't deliberately trying to get pregnant. When I'd thought that he would be upset when I told him, I was also right, but upset was an understatement. It was clear that he was panicking, but more than anything he was *angry* with me. He was *seriously* angry.

"I'm not ready to have a kid. You're just trying to trap me," he said.

I was alarmed by the almost tangible anger in his response and hurt by his accusations. Here I was, pregnant with his child, and instead of celebrating he was spewing insults at me and accusing me of being malicious. He ordered me to get an abortion and I went to the doctor to book the appointment. I had to prepare myself to go to the TPU (Termination of

Pregnancy Unit) again. Aside from Carma and my girls, only Carma's brother knew about my pregnancy. He and I began texting. He told me that he didn't think Carma and I were ready but he supported my decision either way.

The night before my scheduled abortion, I said aloud what I'd been holding in my heart the entire time.

"I don't want to have an abortion," I said to my friend Serena, who had agreed to accompany me.

"So don't," she said.

I looked at her strangely. It hadn't occurred to me to keep the baby against Carma's will.

"I can't. Carma will be even madder than he already is," I said. Visions of him beating me into a miscarriage ran through my mind.

"I can't," I said again. There was *no way* I was going against his orders. Plus, I'd already told him that I wouldn't keep it. "The appointment is already booked," I told her.

"So don't go," she said again. She scrunched her eyebrows together in defiance.

I cringed at how that conversation would go if I told Carma I wasn't going through with the abortion. I didn't want him to resent me. I didn't want him to *hate* me! In a sense, I knew it was my decision but all I was concerned about was what *Carma* would think. I was confused.

I decided to call Meghan. My sister said the same thing that Serena did, only she explained herself. "It's your baby. At the end of the day, he can't force you to have an abortion. If he didn't want you to get pregnant, he shouldn't have been having sex with you without a condom. Plus, you know we'll be here to help you the same way we helped Quin. Whatever you decide, I still love you, but if you want to keep it then keep it."

I told her that it wasn't that easy but she insisted that it was. "That's his own business if he doesn't want to be in his child's life. If he wants to be a deadbeat dad then you don't need him," she said. We got off the phone.

A sense of hope sparked in me that gave me the confidence to tell Carma that I wanted to keep the baby. The doctor had confirmed that I was two months and two days pregnant. I didn't know exactly what that meant in terms of the baby's development but the baby had already begun to make my body react and I didn't want to get rid of it. My sister had assured me that I would have support and I felt that was all I needed, even if it wasn't coming from Carma. I texted her and told her that I was going to keep it.

Let me know how it goes when you tell Carma. I'm happy for you sister! Oh my god, you're gonna have a baby! she replied.

The next thing I did was text my homegirl Keisha, who was Carma's cousin's girlfriend. She said exactly what Meghan had said. I was happy to have their support and to know that I wasn't doing anything wrong by keeping the baby.

And so, I called Carma.

When I told him that I wanted to keep the baby, anger struck him again. And again, he accused me of trapping him. "So, what, I don't get any say in this?" he asked.

I was quiet. I felt like he was right. Mentally, I knew it took two to make a baby but emotionally I felt like he was right in saying that I was forcing him into a situation that he didn't want to be in. There was hatred in his voice. The anger spoke volumes.

"Well, let me know right now if you're keeping it because I have to tell my mom," he said.

It wasn't so much that he was giving me the opportunity to make the decision myself as it was a guilt trip. He asked me how I planned to support the baby and where I was going to live. I obviously had no answers to these questions. The little bit of hope and confidence I had in my decision had vanished.

"All right then, I won't keep it," I told him. My eyes filled with tears. We got off the phone and I openly cried while Serena lay beside me. "I can't do it. I can't bring a baby into this world if it's not wanted," I sobbed. The next morning, Serena and I rode in silence to the hospital in a taxi.

I cried that whole morning. The intake process was all too familiar. The nurse took my blood pressure, I was given a hospital gown, I signed some papers. The nurse asked if this was my first abortion and I had to say no. Still crying, I was asked *that* question again: Is someone making you do this? I shook my head to say no. Whether or not the nurse believed me, I don't know, but I don't think it was her job to determine whether I was lying or telling the truth.

I was very anxious lying on the operating table. My nerves were shot and I couldn't stay still. One of the doctors stood behind my head with her hands on my shoulders trying to get me to relax. This had not happened during my first abortion. My legs trembled as the other doctor positioned herself in between my legs. She explained the procedure to me but I didn't hear her. Tears fell from my eyes and rolled down the sides of my face into my ears.

"Jade, I need you to calm down, honey," said the doctor above my head. The doctor between my legs turned on the machine that was going to take my baby from me. I cried out loud. Inside, my heart was screaming, "No!" The procedure began anyway. My belly felt like it was rumbling as the suction tube ripped my baby from its growing place.

"We're almost done," the doctor said. Unlike the first abortion, this one was extremely painful. I felt everything.

It was more than uncomfortable. It was more than a medical procedure. It was murder. I was killing the child that I had wanted. It was like regret invaded my lungs. Suddenly, I couldn't breathe. I started gasping for air. As if it was never real to begin with, I was no longer pregnant. All of my dreams of being a mother and having a family now sat at the bottom of a medically approved vacuum.

"Jade, I need you to calm down. I have to scrape your uterus to ensure that I removed all of the tissue," the doctor told me. My breathing started to return to normal, then it slowed to a strange pace. Mentally, I left before the surgical tool could even enter me. I was no longer in my body, no longer in the operating room. I couldn't watch this happen. I don't know where I went but I was not there anymore.

After the procedure was finished, I was guided into the recovery room. I felt like a little old woman the way my back hunched, and I slowly walked to the room with the nurse's hands on my wrist and shoulder. I was told to put on a pad so that they could monitor my bleeding. I didn't care if I bled to death and I kind of hoped that I would. Nothing mattered anymore. The life was sucked from my womb and whatever life I had in me was gone.

In my mind, I'd had my child killed. *It's your fault!* I repeated to myself inside my head. I was angry at the doctors and angry at myself. I started to lose my breath again. This time, hysteria invaded my lungs. Insanity rushed through me. I needed to scream — at the doctors, myself . . . the world. Instead of screaming, I bawled my eyes out.

The women around me remained silent. A nurse approached me with some type of medication in her hand, asking if I wanted something to help me calm down. She called it "the happy pill." It was small and blue. I couldn't find my voice to answer her question. I forced my eyes open but they were empty, a hollow vase of vision. I extended my hand to accept her offer. Within a few minutes, I stopped crying. The ache in my heart faded to black. I fell asleep.

I awoke to the nurse nudging my shoulder. It was time to check my pad again to see if I was bleeding normally. Afterward they said I was free to go.

Carma came to pick me up. We didn't talk much on the way back to where I was still staying with Daneen and her family. He dropped me off and said he had to do something but that he would be back later.

I was still angry. My heart was still angry. I went into my room, not wanting to be bothered by anyone. The cramps in my stomach were unlike any I'd experienced before. I lay in my bed, adopting the fetal position. I couldn't bear the pain. I cried to myself.

A couple of hours later, Carma came back. He'd brought me a strawberry sundae from McDonald's.

"I hate to see you in so much pain," he said.

He sat on the edge of my bed and rubbed my back before he lay down beside me, with his back against my headboard. He put my head in his lap. Cramps shot through my belly and sharp pains ran through my back. I shuddered.

"Even I felt that one," he said.

I don't remember what we talked about as we lay there. Eventually he left and I was alone again. I grabbed some Tylenol 3 from the kitchen cabinet and drifted back into sleep.

* * *

A month later, I celebrated my nineteenth birthday. One of

my girl friends had a party for me at her house and I invited a bunch of people there to drink and have a good time. It was that night that I wanted the presence of my mother for the first time in a long time. I called her and told her to come to the party and when she was taking too long, I walked to her house and burst through her door just as she was putting on her shoes. She started cracking up laughing at how drunk I was.

Carma was at the party too. We smoked weed and drank until we were silly drunk. When Zee arrived, I went to greet him and his friend at the door. His friend wished me a happy birthday and went inside. Zee grabbed me up in a hug and kissed me deeply. I squirmed and then kissed him back. As we went inside, I was blushing really hard, attempting to be alert to Carma's whereabouts. Zee went left and I went right and nearly knocked Carma over. My actions could probably be read on my face.

"Don't think I don't know," he said.

"Know what?" I asked. I laughed and walked away and he didn't pursue the conversation any further.

Carma ended up leaving early, so I went on hosting my party and flirting with some of the guys who were there. I popped a Molly to hype up my night even more. I was nineteen! I wanted this to be the party of all parties!

It was after 4 a.m. when everyone finally left. My girls were ready to call it quits but I was still in party mode. The Molly had me wide awake.

"Jade, go to bed! You're gonna be so tired tomorrow, you're gonna sleep your whole birthday away!" they said.

I told them I was fine and to leave me alone.

They insisted that I needed to get some sleep. "You're not fine!" Serena nearly yelled at me.

I grabbed up the six Advil Liqui-Gels off the dresser and shoved them in my mouth.

"What the fuck, Jade!" Now Serena was yelling. "Oh my god, this girl just took six Advil!" she said.

I stumbled over to the bed and sat down. I don't know what I was trying to prove by taking the Advil. Everyone was going crazy, not knowing what to do. After arguing that I was fine, I decided to leave.

"It's my birthday, bitches!" I kept saying. They gave up on trying to persuade me and let me leave.

I called Carma and told him to come pick me up from this girl's house that I knew who lived a block away. It was 6 a.m. by this time, but it was my birthday so he got out of his bed and came anyway.

I talked his head off the whole way back to his house in North Preston, which was a twenty-five-minute drive. "Those bitches tried to tell me to go to bed. It's my birthday!" I told him.

"You're high, ain't ya," he said.

I smiled and told him that I was. He said he wouldn't say anything because it was my birthday.

When we got to his house, he wanted to go to sleep but I wanted to have sex. I dug in his drawer for a condom. When I looked in his drawer, I swore up and down that a condom was missing. I accused him of cheating on me. I started freaking out and yelling at him. He told me to be quiet because his parents were upstairs. I don't know if it was because I was high or because I was upset but suddenly I couldn't breathe.

I called my mom, of all people, and yelled at her through the phone that I was "gonna fuck Carma up" because a condom was missing. My mom had no idea what I was talking about so she gave the phone to Meghan.

"Jade, what are you talking about?" she laughed.

I explained it to her.

"Uh, uh! Just try to enjoy the rest of your birthday. Don't worry about the condom right now," she said.

I hung up and went back to argue with Carma.

"Just come to bed, please. Get some sleep. I have a plan for us for your birthday so get some sleep," Carma said.

I finally gave in and laid down for an hour or two until I made him get up again.

He celebrated my birthday with me by driving to a neighbouring city. I think it was Truro. We drove for nearly an hour until we found a motel. He took me out to eat at Jungle Jim's and I ordered a huge meal that I couldn't finish. The dish was called "Everything under the Kitchen Sink." It had a bunch of different meats. Afterward, we grabbed a bottle of liquor and went back to the hotel. We had planned to get dressed up and find a little bar or club to go to but both of us got horny and ended up going to bed. We made love until we got tired and fell asleep. The next morning, we headed back to the city.

Carma was turning nineteen just over a month after I did. It was somewhere between my birthday and his that I broke up with him (again). I'd been resenting him since the abortion. I still wanted to build a life with him — to be his wife, business partner and the mother of his child. Despite the roller coaster that we always seemed to be on, I was his and I wanted him to be mine and only mine. But it all felt so far away. He'd already said that he wasn't ready for a child.

Often he'd say, "You gotta stay down to come up." This meant that I had to put in the work and time necessary to secure my future with him. Up until then, I had been down for that. I had always been his *ride or die girl*, his *down ass bitch*. The night he told me to have sex with Jaylin in order to prove my loyalty to him — I did it. His words from that night echoed in my brain. "You're a real fucking bitch!" he kept repeating. "You're the boss girl; I ain't never leaving you." I'd thought he meant it.

I wanted to believe that he knew how much I loved him and wanted to spend the rest of my life with him but right then it seemed impossible. "He just doesn't understand," I told Cadence. She had always been my voice of reason — my connection to the outside world, to reality. It was her who ignited a series of firsts (attempts to leave). She reminded me of my worth. She faithfully remained in the backdrop of my complicated life, offering support and a listening ear whenever I needed it. I had kept her separate, not only because of that but because Carma didn't like her. On the rare occasion that I did speak her name around him, he would always claim that she was stuck up. "I don't want to hear about that girl. She don't know how to speak," he'd say. What he was really saying was that she didn't go out of her way to initiate a conversation with him, like some other girls would and that he was offended by that.

The memories of the previous four years of my life weighed heavy on my heart, specifically the night Carma and I discussed the STI that I had contracted. In my heart, I could still see the colour leave his eyes. It looked as if he'd left himself, the same way I had done while servicing my clients in the dimly lit rooms of the massage parlour. I conveyed this memory to Cadence. I was tired. I was so, so tired and I told her that too.

"Listen, Jade. I know you probably don't want to hear this but I'm going to say it anyway, as your friend. Carma is going to kill you one day. The way you just explained that situation sounds like he doesn't know his own strength and

I feel like one day he could kill you. Even if he doesn't, you have to understand that until you leave him alone, he will never be the man that you want him to be. He's not capable of doing that right now. He's too busy chasing money. You have to leave him so he can understand that you're not just going to take all of his bullshit. One day he's going to look back and see that you're the only girl who ever really loved him and he's going to regret how he treated you. Maybe one day he'll come back and apologize and maybe then you guys can build a life together but right now, that's not going to happen. You need to leave him, Jade," Cadence said.

Finally, it clicked. I knew she was right. It hurt like hell. Everything I'd worked for meant nothing. Everything I'd worked for was about to go down the drain, but I knew she was right.

"I'm gonna leave him," I told her.

"Good. Are you gonna call him or text him?" she asked.

"I'm gonna text him first 'cause I don't know how he's gonna respond. He's probably gonna go crazy," I said.

"Okay, boo. Call me back after you talk to him and let me know what he says," she replied.

I hung up the phone and took a deep breath. *I can't do this,* I told myself. *I love him so, so much.* I hung my head in defeat, thinking about the baby I'd murdered — the same baby who would be his first born child. I was convinced the baby was a girl — I knew she was gone but I still felt her there. I still needed her to mend the broken pieces of my failed relationship. But he didn't want her.

It was time. I knew it was time. I opened up our message thread and started to type out my escape.

Carma, I can't be with you anymore . . .

EPILOGUE

If you're telling yourself there's no way that I broke up with him just like that then you're absolutely right. I didn't. Our relationship status changed but we still stayed connected. As strongly as I felt in the moment that it was the end, it wasn't, not yet. He wasn't about to let me walk away and I'm not entirely sure I wanted to. In fact, I didn't want to at all, but I felt like I had no other choice — as I'd often felt in other situations involving Carma. You don't just walk away from someone you love overnight — at least not emotionally and mentally. Even without our official relationship status, I continued to experience abuse at what seemed to be his leisure — plus, we were still involved sexually, which made letting go even more complicated. Though not my first partner, he was all I knew. The way I related to Carma following that breakup could continue to be told for another two years or so. It took that long, coupled with another seemingly endless series of ups and downs, to finally rid myself of him. It was years before I was just "Jade" and not "Carma's girl" or "the one that used to be with Carma."

I am currently four years removed from that relationship. I'm twenty-five now and it baffles me to be the woman that I am now compared to the teenager that I was all of those years ago. Not only because I made it through that part of my life but also because, for years after, I had no desire to start anew on my own. I was very lost and certainly misguided. I just wanted to forget about everything that had happened. Unfortunately, I don't get to. Yes, I can repress memories when they arise but there will always be reminders. Like when I'm on Facebook and one of our mutual friends posts his picture and I see that smile of his. Or now that I live in Toronto, sometimes I'll be riding the bus and cruise past the massage parlour where I used to work. There are some things, although they are minor details, that will always cause memories to come flooding back. I don't hate him but it was years before I reached a place of forgiveness.

The journey of getting back to myself or better yet, creating a new me was . . . a long one. I plan to detail that process in my next book.

I know that this book can and will be refuted, possibly for generations to come. I cannot stop that. I have written with my purest efforts. I have had to be honest about parts of myself that I have never spoken out loud until now. If I had the energy for debate, I would ask doubters what it would serve me to lie. Telling this story does not get back those years of my life. It doesn't put him in jail and I have no desire for him to be there. I'm not here for that. I'm here using my story to serve as my justice by giving back to a world that I feel I took so much from. Beyond what I've explained here, I refuse to try to convince anyone of its authenticity.

A piece of advice I want to give to my fellow survivors and any other person able to relate to the various methods of manipulation and abuse that I've detailed here: Know yourself! As cliché and simple as it sounds, it has been the defining factor of surviving myself. When I was with Carma, I had no real identity of my own. I was who he told me to be and who I thought he wanted me to be. It wasn't until I made the decision to figure out who I was as an individual that I began to live, deciding which labels and lifestyles I would adhere to. I encourage you to do the same, whatever that looks like for you. I have a ton of cliché quotes that I could share with you for motivation for your self-realization, but mostly I want you to know that I love you for surviving thus far and if nobody has told you this yet, I believe you.

I believe you.

ACKNOWLEDGEMENTS

I knew the universe had aligned for me when publisher Jim Lorimer told me how he'd found me. Major thanks to the staff at Formac for this collaboration and for all of the work that went into perfecting my manuscript, especially the editing team!

For my friend who initiated the writing of this book, with love but also annoying persistence, thank you tenfold. Had you not known that I had a story to tell, had you not known that this story could save someone's life, this book would have never come to fruition. At the very least, it has saved *my* life.

To my love and co-creator, thank you for listening. Thank you for all of your logic and advice, even when I didn't want to hear it. You helped me make sense of it all. I love you so much.

How do you thank your friends for their part in your legacy when they're all so phenomenal? There will never be enough words to describe you. I am so grateful. Your support and excitement during this process was often the confidence boost I needed to continue. Thank you for allowing me to be my true self, regardless of who that self was.

Mom and Dad, you are forgiven. Please, forgive yourselves every day and every minute that you need to. I love you. I am still your miracle.

For every perpetrator of violence in my life, in the words of Kurt Cobain, "Thank you for the tragedy, I need it for my art."

ABOUT THE AUTHOR

JADE H. BROOKS, now in her mid-twenties, lives with her family on Canada's west coast. As an advocate against human trafficking, Jade uses her life experiences to raise awareness and prevent young people from being coerced into the sex trade. She holds a college diploma in Community Services.